The Merlin EH(AW) 101
From Design to Front Line

RICH PITTMAN

AMBERLEY

Official roll-out of the EH101, with the then state-of-the-art multi-coloured lights and smoke machine. 7 April 1987. (Photo: Leonardo Helicopters)

First published 2017

Amberley Publishing
The Hill, Stroud,
Gloucestershire, GL5 4EP

www.amberley-books.com

ISBN 978 1 4456 7436 0 (print)
ISBN 978 1 4456 7437 7 (ebook)

British Library Cataloguing in Publication Data.
A catalogue record for this book is available from the British Library.

Typeset in 10pt on 13pt Celeste.
Typesetting by Amberley Publishing.
Printed in the UK.

Contents

Foreword

The initial concept for the EH101 was for an anti-submarine warfare helicopter. During the helicopter's lifespan this design brief has grown and developed. Today, what is now the AW101 is a multi-role aircraft offering an advanced solution for military, government and heads of state transportation.

Recently the AW101 has been adapted into a flexible multi-role platform for Search and Rescue (SAR) and Combat Search and Rescue (CSAR) operations.

The AW101's airborne endurance and size make it ideal for long-range missions, capable of delivering or extracting a large number of civilians, troops or casualties in difficult locations.

My career as a test pilot with Westland Helicopters began in 1979. I became Deputy Chief Test Pilot in 1986 and became Chief Test Pilot in 1988. You typically only get the one chance in your career as a test pilot to bring a new aircraft into service. Bringing the EH101 Merlin from the initial proposal, through pre-production development and then to oversee the introduction into service and distribution to customers was a great honour. On 9 October 1987, Westland Chief Test Pilot Trevor Egginton and myself made the first short flight of the EH101 Merlin.

When I see the current Merlin flying about today in the skies over Somerset, I look up and think of all the tests, trials and tribulations we completed in the 1980s and 90s. Then I think, 'I wish I was up there today,' flying with the current servicemen and women of the Royal Navy.

The text and the photographs in this book tell the story of the Merlin and its many achievements during the past thirty years. It's full of fascinating facts and figures about this aircraft and I am sure it will appeal to a wide audience.

I am so delighted Rich has had the initiative to document this project's development. Enjoy *The Merlin EH(AW) 101: From Design to Front Line.*

Colin Hague OBE
Chief Test Pilot
Westland Helicopters
1988–2003

Acknowledgments

Assembling a book on the EH(AW) 101 Merlin was, as one might expect, a difficult task to be achieved by one person. The author was obliged to rely on many individuals, and this book would not have been possible without their support and research. In no particular order I would like to thank the following people and organisations.

Amberley Publishing
Leonardo Helicopters
Colin Hague OBE
Ian Harding
Dave Langrish
Jon Coombes
Dave Burrow
Mick Burrow
Nichola Pittman
Chris Shaw
Royal Canadian Air Force
Lt Col Carita & CAP Gouevia
Liam Daniels
Robin A. Walker
Joe Copalman
Paul Harvey
Jorge Ruivo
Niels Roman
Robin Coenders
David Ellins
Russell Ayre
Mick Holland
Domenico Marchi
Tony Osborne
Mark Munzel

David Cenciotti, 'The Aviationist'
Trustees of the RAF Museum
Mark Service
www.ukserials.com
www.targetlock.org.uk

I would like to dedicate this book to my late father, Anthony Richard Pittman. Tony worked at Westland's for twenty-eight years and his job was the reason we relocated to Yeovil. The Merlin and Westland's have played a very large part of keeping the town of Yeovil and the surrounding area prosperous.

Parts of this book (Portugal, Norway, HC.4, HM.2 and Crowsnest) are copyright and reproduced with the kind permission of Ian Harding.

Every attempt has been made to seek permission for copyright material used in the book. If we have inadvertently used copyright material without permission or acknowledgement we apologise and will make the necessary correction at the first opportunity.

All photographs copyright Rich Pittman unless stated.

CHAPTER ONE

Introduction

The threat of an attack by Soviet missile submarines was judged as a serious threat to UK assets in the 1970s and '80s and the UK Ministry of Defence issued a requirement for a new type of helicopter to be developed during 1977 to counter the issue.

Initially the Westland WG-34 was proposed to be the replacement for the WS-61 Sea King. It was planned to be a three-engine helicopter of similar proportions to the Sea King, but the WG-34 was designed to feature more cabin space and have a greater operating range than its predecessor. At that time, the Italian Navy was also considering a successor for its fleet of SH-3D Sea Kings, which had been manufactured locally by the Italian company Agusta. Subsequently Westland (UK) and Agusta (Italy) entered into negotiations regarding a joint-development of the future helicopter. After the companies finalised an agreement to work on the project together, a jointly owned company called European Helicopter Industries Limited (EHI) was formed to provide the development and marketing of the new helicopter to potential customers. The EHI-01 emerged as the collaborative design, but a clerical error in retyping hand-written notes during early draft stages accidently renamed the helicopter as EH101 and the name was adopted.

On 12 June 1981, the UK government confirmed its participation in the project and initially allocated £20 million toward development of the programme. By 1984, a key agreement followed, signed by the British and Italian governments, which secured funding for the majority of the EH101's development.

An international marketing survey highlighted a requirement for a thirty-seat helicopter. Following the original concept of a replacement naval anti-submarine warfare (ASW) aircraft, EHI decided to develop the EH101 into a multirole platform. As a medium-lift helicopter, the aircraft would be able to meet the demands of utility, government and civilian corporations of the 1990s. An initial nine pre-production (PP) models were produced to demonstrate these potential configurations to the worldwide market. As design studies progressed, it was decided that transport versions should also be developed, leading ultimately to a number of different EH101 variants being proposed and developed.

During July 2000, Agusta and Westland Helicopters formally amalgamated to become AgustaWestland. As a consequence, the consortium name, EH Industries, was consigned

Artist impressions of the civilian and naval EH101.

to history. The EH101 became known as the AW101 from 2007 onwards. A new chapter in the aircraft's history had commenced.

This book has been created to celebrate and showcase the development of the AW101 as it approaches its thirtieth anniversary on 9 October 2017. It also reflects upon the important phases of its history to date, including design, development, manufacture, technology, agility, adaptability and enhanced capabilities going forward.

CHAPTER TWO

Design

The design requirement for the EH101 included enhanced safety, maintainability, mission and operational capability. The design criteria included three engines and maximum use of composites to reduce weight allied to improved fatigue properties; a design that would also reduce pilot workload, have higher reliability and offer all-weather capability, producing a safe, reliable and cost-effective medium-lift helicopter. The collaborative structure, being a 50/50 partnership, actually had no specific design-leader from the outset – possibly an unthinkable situation in today's industry?

The initial design of the EH101 took place in the early 1980s and followed a conventional design layout, but making use of advanced technologies, such as the design of the rotor blades, avionics systems, and the extensive use of composite materials. Implemented from late on in the pre-production stage, the fuselage structure would comprise a recently commercialised aluminium-lithium alloy, designed to be both light and damage-resistant. The aluminium-lithium Alloy AA8090 could achieve significant weight savings of around 10 per cent over previously used alloys, resulting in an inherent lower-density material with the bonus of an increased elastic modulus. This alloy would eventually account for over 90 per cent of all aluminium alloy used in construction of the airframe.

The original power plant selected for the pre-production aircraft was the General Electric CT7-401A, which would later be changed to Rolls-Royce engines at the customer's request.

The EH101 would be fitted with composite blades utilising glass and carbon fibres woven and bonded together. These blades were also manufactured with new special shaped tips, which were developed from the British Experimental Rotor Programme (BERP). The five main-rotor BERP blades featured swept tips, which allowed the helicopter to fly at high speed without suffering from the problems of blade stall while also providing an increased lift-capacity over previous conventional blades. Following the BERP development, Westland's own Lynx demonstrator (G-LYNX) in its modified form took to the air from Yeovil on 11 August 1986 with Westland's Chief Test Pilot, Trevor Egginton, at the controls and Flight Test Engineer Derek Clews alongside. Flying a 9.3-mile course over the Somerset Levels, G-LYNX reached 249.09 mph (400 km/h), smashing the 'Hind's' best figure (228.9 mph, September 1978) to set up a new Class E (Rotorcraft) Absolute

A mock-up EH101, displayed at the Farnborough Air Show, 1988. (Photo: Robin A. Walker)

World Speed Record that remains unbroken to this day. It was in effect a technology demonstrator for the larger scale EH101 that was about to break cover.

When the EH101 emerged in 1987, it would feature the most advanced avionics systems and aerodynamics package ever for an ASW platform. The aircraft also managed to deliver a multi-purpose helicopter with a spacious cabin that could accommodate up to thirty passengers, the most-advanced armaments available and up to twenty-four fully equipped combat troops. When required, the EH101 can also be converted to carry sixteen stretchers for military casualty evacuation (CASEVAC) or humanitarian and disaster relief operations and still fly for up to 5 hours with three-engine safety and flexibility, yet only weigh 31,500 lbs!

CHAPTER THREE

Preparing for Take Off

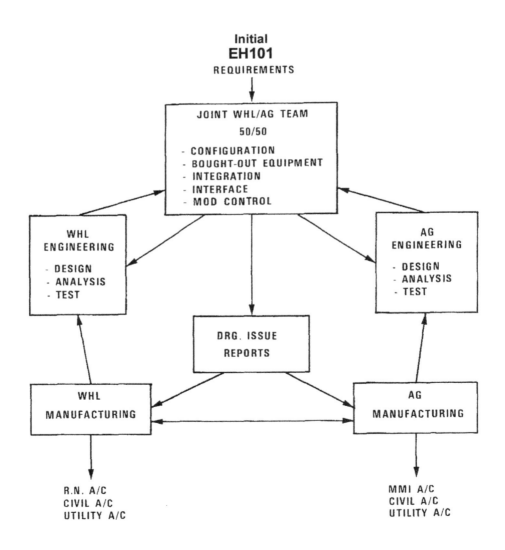

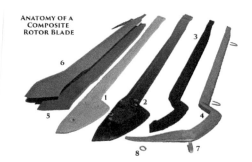

ANATOMY OF A COMPOSITE ROTOR BLADE

1- FOAM MAIN SPAR
2- +/- 45 DEGREE AND UNIDIRECTIONAL COMPOSITE MATERIAL
3- HEATER MAT
4- EROSION SHIELD
5- NOMEX HONEYCOMB TRAILING EDGE CORE
6- TRAILING EDGE CARBON FIBRE SKINS
7- TIP BALANCE WEIGHTS
8- TITANIUM STRAPS

With confirmation of the funding agreed and secured in 1984 for development of the Anglo-Italian EH101, work to bring the components together for the first pre-production (PP1) aircraft commenced in both countries. Hardware was exchanged between the consortium partners, who shared the design phase equally. The assembly of airframe PP1 commenced using major module components at the Westland manufacturing facility in Yeovil, Somerset, UK. The tail pylon and stabiliser modules arrived in the UK from Agusta in Italy and they also supplied the transmission units. In a reciprocal move, Westland sent a forward fuselage complete with glazing structure and a main cabin section to Italy for PP2, Italy's first PP aircraft and the second aircraft to fly during the development phase. Production moved at pace with Westland achieving production standard for the composite main rotor blade after bonding only nine blades!

During the construction of the first PP helicopters, Westland and Agusta completed many months of tests and trials at their manufacturing facilities in both Yeovil and at Cascina Costa, Italy. These were essential to demonstrate the suitability of the innovative materials and components used in the new-build EH101, enabling assured progress toward making its first flight.

An initial eight-week programme of airframe tests took place using accurate scale models in water tank test facilities at the Westland Aerospace division in Cowes on the Isle of White in Hampshire, UK. These tests were necessary to prove that the helicopter could make an emergency water landing and be able to survive the sea-state parameters set out in the initial requirements for the helicopter.

Agusta provided ground-based airframes used for fatigue and avionics testing, including a Ground Test Vehicle (GTV) rig. They also commissioned an advanced gearbox test cell, drop-test rig for landing gear and various rigs for exhaustive testing of the fuel, hydraulic, electrical and other systems. All these measures resulted in one of the largest collaborative test programmes undertaken for a new helicopter, ensuring the EH101 entered pre-production and into service as a highly developed aircraft.

As the early project definition stages progressed, further 'lead-in' test activities were undertaken in order to provide basic design information for the new materials and processes.

During the early phase of the 'lead-in' test programme, the GTV known as the 'Iron Bird' was used extensively. Iron Bird consisted of a concrete-based, iron structure, onto which the rear fuselage and pylon sections were attached. This rig was used to commence

Left: A pre-production EH101 at an early stage of assembly. (Photo: Leonardo Helicopters)

Below: Work progressing on a pre-production EH101. (Photo: Leonardo Helicopters)

The 'Iron Bird' ground test vehicle at Cascina Costa, Italy. (Photo: Leonardo Helicopters)

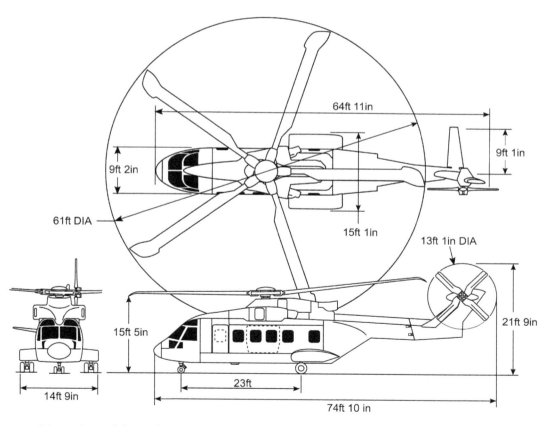

Dimensions of the Utility EH101.

transmission testing ahead of the flying airframe construction, giving prior clearance for the pre-production aircraft to operate.

Iron Bird also provided development of the total drive system, including engine installations, rotors and controls. The full test instrumentation system allowed collection of all significant data parameters, measuring stress-loadings, temperature, pressures and vibration both in real-time via a telemetry system and using on-board recording.

Later in the programme, after being extensively modified to be totally representative of an airframe structure, the 'rig' provided a realistic dynamic environment for testing the actual drive system. This ensured the vibration environment and structural deflections were fully representative of the future helicopter. On completion of the basic drive system development and certification testing, the rig was used for maturity testing. Iron Bird continued to support the flight test programme, providing valuable data and early release of flying aircraft following these critical tests.

This ground testing included structural element tests of the composite materials used for the rotor blades and tests of fasteners and bonding of composite materials used on the aircraft structure. Westland sent a delegation to Agusta to work alongside and complement the Italian personnel involved in the programme.

Initial flight-testing was supported by 'Hack' aircraft, as they became known. These were two Westland Sea Kings in the UK, which were used for radar and avionics development, while in Italy an Agusta ASH-3D tested the sonar systems for the Italian Navy examples.

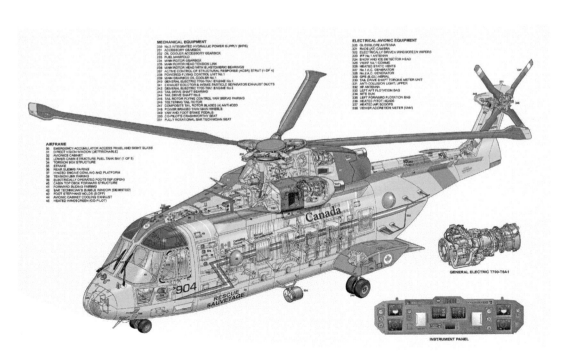

A cutaway illustration, showing off the Canadian CH-149 Cormorant advanced features.

One of the British examples used was Sea King Mk 2 XZ570, being one of Westland's development fleet aircraft. This was used as an early test-bed for the evaluation and development of avionic equipment for the EH101. This aircraft took part in many trials including a three phased exercise:

Phase 1 - Navigation Sensor Evaluation;
Phase 2 - Radar Development;
Phase 3 - Integrated Mission System Evaluation.

The aircraft was extensively modified to carry the Ferranti Blue Kestrel radar and the EH101 mission system.

Another major feature of this early flight phase was the development of a rotor blade de-icing system using a Wessex Mk 5, XT768. A series of trials produced the fundamental design information necessary for the EH101 blade de-icing system. The Wessex was fitted with an advanced rotor head and tail cone cameras to take photos during each flight. These recorded the ice build-up and dispersal, which could then be matched with the data gathered from outside the aircraft for various air conditions and aircraft performance.

Vibration is an ever-present problem in helicopters. Many measures have been tested and adopted in an attempt to reduce or absorb vibration, with varying degrees of success. Vibration causes fatigue in structure, air-crew and passengers. It is also a major source of unreliability in avionics. Westland developed an Active Control of Structural Response (ACSR) system. ACSR took a different approach to the problem. Active control technology was used to feed cancelling loads into hydraulically powered flexible elements in the main gearbox support struts. An active control technique had commenced development on the WG30, being demonstrated in-flight during early 1987.

Initially the power plant selected for the PP aircraft was the General Electric CT7-401A. The UK government announced during the Farnborough Air Show in 1988 that following pre-production testing, the Rolls-Royce-developed Turbomeca RTM322 engine had been selected to power the Royal Navy order.

Westland Hack
Sea King XZ570,
extensively modified
to carry the Ferranti
Blue Kestrel radar.
(Photo: Leonardo
Helicopters)

CHAPTER FOUR

Pre-Production (PP) Years

Using the nine prototypes, an EH101 Integrated Development Programme (IDP) was established. The program was scheduled to include 4,000 hours of initial flight testing. The nine PP aircraft (five built in Britain, and four in Italy) were configured in a series of different versions:

Series 100: Basic Naval;
Series 200: Naval Utility, without the rear loading ramp;
Series 300: 'Heliliner' commercial passenger carrier;
Series 400: Army transport;
Series 500: Civil Utility variant with rear loading ramp.

The first pre-production aircraft, PP1, officially rolled out of the Yeovil Westland factory on 7 April 1987. As a basic development aircraft, PP1 started a 25-hour pre-flight ground testing programme on 9 June. The majority of this pre-flight programme demonstrated the freedom from ground resonance. Ground resonance is an imbalance in the rotation of a helicopter rotor when the blades become bunched up on one side of their rotation plane, which causes an oscillation in phase with the frequency of the helicopter rocking on its landing gear.

PP1 made its maiden flight on 9 October 1987, with Westland's Chief Test-Pilot Trevor Egginton and Deputy Chief Test-Pilot Colin Hague completing a short hover-test. The tail-rotor ground instrumentation failed, preventing the ground crew from recording the stress-load on the tail rotor, thereby curtailing its first flight as a precaution.

The first two aircraft, PP1 in the UK and PP2 in Italy, were primarily tasked with basic airworthiness clearance for the helicopter. Within the first 45 hours of flying, PP1 had flown at 140 knots up to an altitude of 10,000ft, carried out 45-degree banked turns and taken off with the maximum expected naval all-up weight. A review took place at 50 flying hours and the statistics for PP1 and PP2 included flight at 150 knots at the design weight of 28,660 lbs; during the early stage of IDP, it was decided to temporally move PP1 to Italy with the more favourable Mediterranean climate. PP1 flew to Avonmouth Docks in Bristol for transportation by boat. Upon reaching Italy, the rotors were refitted, checks were made and PP1 completed its journey by flying on to Cascina Costa, joining PP2.

PP1 conducting the very intensive ground resonance trials, continuing into the night. (Photo: Leonardo Helicopters)

Trevor Eggington and Colin Hague take the first EH101 prototype on its maiden flight, 9 October 1987. (Photo: Leonardo Helicopters)

With the basic flight testing complete by January 1991, PP1 was given the serial ZF641 while engaging in further military trials. ZF641 was tested on Defence Test and Evaluation Organisation (DTEO) Boscombe Down's Rolling Platform Facility during the summer of 1997. The Rolling Platform Facility simulates ship motion, enabling the development and testing of a variety of systems and equipment for use at sea. These tests included the reliability for the automatic blade and tail folding mechanisms in the (simulated) worst sea states that the helicopter was designed to operate in. ZF641 was then transferred to RNAS Culdrose during July 1998 for further ground handling trials. Aircraft handlers at Culdrose were able to simulate real-life situations, using the life-size HMS *Invincible* class flight deck mock-up on land, known as a 'Dummy Deck'.

PP2 made its first flight shortly after PP1, on 26 November 1987, and was given the Italian serial MMX-600 during IDP. PP2 was involved with deck-landing trials on the Italian Navy ships INS *Grecale* and INS *Maestrale* during July 1990. On 21 January 1993,

PP2's history was cut short during an acoustic measurement test when it crashed and was destroyed near Novara-Cameri in Italy, sadly killing all four crew on board. The ensuing crash investigation concluded the crash had been caused by an un-commanded application of the rotor-brake causing an in-flight fire.

PP3 was developed as a civil commercial 'Heliliner' variant prototype. Built at Westland in Yeovil, it completed its first flight on 30 September 1988 and boasted a new engine design, the GE CT7-6/6A. The PP3 flight-test programme included engine vibration tests followed by weapons carriage tests with the military serial ZH647 allocated. It also conducted icing trials at Canadian Force Base Shearwater, Canada, during 1993. Subsequently, PP3 was grounded on 12 February 1999 having completed 581 flights and a total flight time of 653 hours. Following the removal of essential spares it was stored at the Yeovil factory before being donated to the Helicopter Museum at Weston-super-Mare on 26 November 1999.

PP4 was built as a basic development British naval prototype fitted with a fully integrated and functioning avionics suite. The first flight took place on 15 June 1989 and this airframe was used to conduct over-water navigation system trials and AFCS (Automatic Flight

Italy's first-built EH101 – PP2, a basic variant. (Photo: Leonardo Helicopters)

Part of PP3's testing included an unusual camera fit above the main rotor head to record ice build-up on each of the rotor blades during cold-weather flight trials. (Photo: Leonardo Helicopters)

Control Systems) development. During 1992 the Royal Navy decided on a different engine for their order of the Merlin HM.1; PP4 was selected as one of two aircraft to be retro-fitted with Rolls-Royce Turbomeca RTM322 engines. Many airframes were considered for the RTM322 engine installation, development and integration trials.

An early photo of PP3 with the civil registration G-EHIL applied. (Photo: Leonardo Helicopters)

PP4 with military serial ZF644 on its maiden flight, 15 June 1989. (Photo: Leonardo Helicopters)

Despite this particular helicopter being a joint-asset of Westland and Agusta, PP4, having been built in Yeovil by Westland, was nearing completion of its naval variant systems trials. Following the necessary structural and electrical modifications, PP4 carried out its second maiden flight, this time as an EH101 housing the RTM322 engines, on 6 July 1993, thus beginning a further flight-test programme of 160 hours. PP4, serial ZF644, crashed on 7 April 1995 near the Somerset and Devon border after a drive-train control rod failure. Luckily all four crew members successfully escaped by parachute during its descent before the aircraft was destroyed on impact. ZF644 had flown 385 sorties with a total of 462 flying hours at the time of the incident.

PP5 was a British naval variant built specifically for the future. Constructed at Westland, it first flew on 24 October 1989 and was eventually equipped with dedicated Merlin avionics. Sea-trials commenced, with PP5 carrying the military serial of ZF649. With new Chief Test-Pilot Colin Hague at the controls, the helicopter made its first three deck landings on the Type 23 frigate HMS *Norfolk* (F230). These successful initial deck landings were followed by two weeks of ship interface trials in June 1991. The trials comprised one week of flying activity and one week of exhaustive deck-landings.

PP6 was similarly built to the PP5 specification as a naval variant, but for the Italian Navy this time. Built by Agusta in Italy, it first flew on 26 April 1989. During the PP programme it operated with the pseudo-military serial MMX-605.

PP7 was the military utility variant with a rear loading ramp. It made its maiden flight on 18 December 1989 at Cascina Costa. Nearly seven years later, on 20 August 1996, it was damaged in an accident when it turned over after the tail rotor drive failed on landing. The helicopter was rebuilt and continued in the IDP. PP7 went on to complete thirty-one test flights in snow and

PP5 overflies HMS *Norfolk*. (Photo: Leonardo Helicopters)

PP6 lands on the Italian aircraft carrier *Giuseppe Garibaldi*. (Photo: Leonardo Helicopters)

After completing 620 flight hours during testing, PP6/MMX-605 is now stored at Luni-Sarzana in Italy. September 2010. (Photo: Domenico Marchi)

ice conditions in Denmark and Shearwater, Nova Scotia. During these flights the aircrew flew in severe weather from the ground level up to 9,400 ft in temperatures ranging from zero to -22°C. By mid-1999, PP7 was sent to Montreal, Canada, where Bombardier Services installed a new sophisticated instrumentation suite. Following this upgrade it went on to complete further cold-weather trials in Shearwater during the winter of 1999 and into 2000.

PP8, the Heliliner civil certification version, was built by Westland and was to be the penultimate aircraft in the PP series. It took to the skies on 24 April 1990 complete with a civil registration, G-0101, and became the company demonstrator for the commercial thirty-seat passenger variant. Meanwhile, PP3 continued flying the main certification programme element.

PP8 was given the military serial ZJ116 in 1995, ready for its military trials work. It was deployed to Brindisi in Italy for extensive flying and reliability trials on 17 March 1996, working alongside PP9. Subsequently, both airframes relocated to Aberdeen, Scotland, on 14 May 1998, using the Scottish airport as a base for further reliability and maintainability trials. In March 2000 PP8 undertook an un-refuelled flight of over 8 hours, simulating a 945-nautical-mile (1,087 miles/1,750 km) Search and Rescue (SAR) mission profile, using 12,125 lbs (5,500 kg) internal fuel-load.

After a total of 3,543 flying hours, PP8 made its final test flight on 23 October 2001. However, its story continued at RAF Brize Norton, Oxfordshire, where it went on to support transportability-trials for the RAF Boeing C-17 Globemaster C.1 transport aircraft, overseen by a joint Lockheed Martin/Agusta Westland 'Team 101'. Utilising a specially designed under-carriage that allowed the landing gear to be retracted on the ground and the helicopter lowered, the main demonstration on 23 October 2002 showcased an actual loading time of less than fifteen minutes, with a total time of less than 2 hours, including preparation and loading. Upon completing its final tests, PP8 was donated by AgustaWestland to the RAF Museum and was transported to Hendon by road in November 2002.

PP7 with military serial ZK101 operating on cold weather trials in Shearwater, Canada. (Photo: Leonardo Helicopters)

PP8 lifting from Westland's, possibly on its first flight. (Photo: Leonardo Helicopters)

With enhanced standards, safety and airliner comfort, the civil EH101 was initially designed to combine all these factors for economical and safe passenger operations. (Photo: Leonardo Helicopters)

PP8 and a British International Helicopter S-61 fly together over St Michael's Mount to mark the thirtieth anniversary of the Penzance – Isles of Scilly helicopter passenger service. (Photo: Leonardo Helicopters)

During 2000, PP8 completed a series of landings on the Armada platform, 160 miles north-east of Aberdeen. (Photo: Leonardo Helicopters)

PP9, built in Italy, was a military utility prototype, painted green and initially flying with registration I-LIOI. This Merlin was also adapted to promote other marketing areas when needed and was displayed at the Farnborough Air show in 1994 in a blue scheme.

A few years later, while operating in the extensive trials with PP8, PP9 became the first EH101 to undertake a transatlantic crossing in 1999. It flew from Aberdeen on 30 August, routing via the Faeroes, Iceland and Godthab in Greenland. PP9 landed at Nunavut, North West Canada, on 1 September. The total flight time was 18 hours, undertaken at a steady 150 knots with an altitude ranging from 300 to 10,100 ft (91.44 to 3,078.48 m). No special preparations were made to the aircraft for the flight, even though temperatures dropped as low as -17°C. This transatlantic crossing provided useful route proving information for future crossings. Once in Canada PP9 visited Quebec, Montreal and Ottawa. PP9 also was also on display at the Nova Scotia International Air Show before making the return flight to the UK at the end of the month.

PP9 returned to Scotland at the end of September after clocking up 110 hours of flying during its trip.

PP9 in an early scheme, serial I-LIOI. (Photo: Leonardo Helicopters)

PP9 in a later colour scheme, serial I-LI0I. (Photo: Leonardo Helicopters)

PP9 painted in a potential SAR colour scheme to promote the EH101 to Canada. (Photo: Leonardo Helicopters)

PP8 and PP9 flew a 6,000-hour intensive flight operations programme, flying simulated sorties to demonstrate the reliability and maintainability performance. (Photo: Leonardo Helicopters)

A busy flight shed, filled with pre-production and future EH101s for the Royal Navy. (Photo: Leonardo Helicopters)

CHAPTER FIVE

Into Service

Initial production orders for the EH101 took place in 1991, with civil certification clearance in the UK and Italy following in 1994. The UK and Italy were the first to order, with interest also coming from a number of countries including Denmark, Canada, Portugal and Japan.

Royal Navy (RN) HM.1/2

From the outset, the Merlin's origins were to fill a naval requirement. It came as no surprise when the RN became the launch customers, with the British MoD placing an initial order for forty-four Merlin HM.1s, to be built at Westland's in 1991.

The first production HM.1 began ground run tests on 2 December 1995, with its maiden flight, flown by Colin Hague, taking place four days later.

The first fully mission-equipped Merlin HM.1, and the second from the production line, RN02/ZH822, first flew on 14 January 1997. As production gathered pace, 700M Naval Air Squadron reformed as the Operational Evaluation Unit (OEU) for the Merlin, based at Royal Naval Air Station (RNAS) Culdrose, Cornwall. As the first Royal Navy Merlin squadron, 700M guided the aircraft's service introduction.

824 Naval Air Squadron (NAS) finished its illustrious front-line career when it reformed as the Merlin training squadron in 2000, with eight aircraft and responsibility for covering all aspects of Merlin operations. 824's objective is to train and convert pilots, observers and aircrew to the Merlin during the conversion course, which lasts approximately forty weeks. On successful completion of the course, aircrew are awarded 'Wings' and sent to front-line squadrons.

814 NAS, 'Flying Tigers', reformed in 2001 with the Merlin HM.1, having been disbanded ten months previously. 814 NAS provided the Merlin with her operational debut. The specialist tactical observers positioned behind the pilots in the cabin enable the aircraft to be flown in any weather conditions by providing radar coverage. Using highly sophisticated tactical mission systems, the aircrew can find and track submarines utilising the aircraft's passive and active sonar systems. Merlins from 814 NAS forward deployed to RNAS Yeovilton during 2012, to provide maritime security during the 2012 London Olympic Games sailing events held in Weymouth, Dorset.

The first production-built Merlin takes to the skies for the first time: ZH821 for the Royal Navy, seen on 6 December 2005. (Photo: Leonardo Helicopters via Colin Hague)

A Royal Navy HM.1 takes off from the threshold of RNAS Yeovilton's main runway.

An 814 NAS Merlin that was forward deployed to RNAS Yeovilton taxiies out to conduct maritime policing and security operations during the Olympic Games in August 2012.

820 NAS, the 'Flying Fish', upgraded from the Sea King to the Merlin in 2003 and operate on the front line alongside 814 NAS. The 'Queens Squadron' will be the primary squadron to operate aboard the Royal Navy's new Queen Elizabeth class aircraft carriers when they enter service, equipped with the Lockheed Martin F-35B Lightning II.

829 NAS, 'the Kingfishers', reestablished on Trafalgar Day in 2004 to provide flights for deployment on Type 23 frigates. While on operational tours, the frigate and helicopter make a great team on maritime surveillance missions, searching for pirates, smugglers and drug-runners, all of which encapsulates the 829 motto, '*non effugient*' – they shall not escape. The squadron also proves support for disaster relief missions, as well as carrying passengers, load lifting plus search and rescue sorties.

With the HM.1 version only just getting 'its feet wet', on 3 June 2003 the UK MoD announced that Lockheed Martin UK Ltd had been selected as preferred contractor on a two-year programme to assess possible upgrades to the Merlin HM.1. Westland Helicopters Ltd would be a strategic sub-contractor in a partnership, which would investigate how to sustain Merlin's capabilities to meet the defence challenges of the next two to three decades.

Almost fifteen years after the first RN Merlin HM.1 entered service in December 1998, a new era of Merlin operations commenced, following the delivery of five HM.2 aircraft to 824 NAS at RNAS Culdrose.

The Merlin Capability Sustainment Programme would provide upgrades to thirty HM.1s, bringing them to the latest HM.2 specification. A production line was set up at Westland's to convert the HM.1 to Mk 2 standard in 2010. This major upgrade programme took approximately nine months to complete and at its peak, the production pulse-line contained

A Royal Navy EH101, on a trials flight operating out of Boscombe Down, conducting a confined area landing, 16 July 2013.

Merlin HM.2 ZH853 flies past St Michael's Mount, Cornwall. (Photo: Ian Harding)

A view from above. A Merlin HM.2 during an Air2Air photo flight. (Photo: Ian Harding)

ten aircraft. New aircraft arrived for conversion approximately every six weeks. Standing alongside its predecessor the HM.1, there are four small external differences distinguishing this next-generation helicopter. Externally the HM.2 looks the same, has the same engines and fundamentally flies the same. That is where comparisons end. It is inside the aircraft where the development work has been done. The HM.2 has been fitted with a modern digital system that addresses every aspect of the aircraft's avionics, new open-architecture tactical missions systems, redesigned cockpit, total re-wiring of the aircraft and enhancements to the radar and sonar systems. Internally, this really is a new helicopter. The Merlin HM.2 represents the culmination of a decade of concept, design, integration and test, ensuring it continues to be the world's most potent submarine hunting helicopter, fit for the needs of today's threats.

Inside the HM.2 you are immediately presented with an array of evolutionary features including a state-of-the-art glass cockpit, improved aircrew console and the very latest in tactical mission systems design, which was critically led by Merlin operators, rather than system specialists. Incorporating the modern open-architecture systems was a key part of the HM.2 internal design, as this offers greater flexibility, making it relatively easy and more cost-effective when additional role equipment such as night vision goggles and enhanced electro-optical/infrared sensors are added. With the latest tactical systems and hardware available to them, the HM.2 two rear crew now have the capability to operate independently, process information at substantially greater speeds, attack multiple targets above and below surface, disseminate this information quickly and present it in a more user-friendly fashion. Central to these key changes are vastly improved Human Machine Interface (HMI) incorporating large flat touch screen panel displays, as well as significant improvements in the radar and sonar systems. However, should the aircraft be required for any of its secondary roles, these modularised consoles can be divided or dismantled, quickly enabling the cabin to be re-configured quickly. The multi-role multi-mission HM.2 has lost none of the previous HM.1's flexibility and in this respect it retains an impressive array of secondary roles.

A Merlin HM.1 lands on the deck of HMS *Bulwark* off the coast of Dorset in August 2012. (Photo: Ian Harding)

The Ministry of Defense took delivery of the final upgraded Merlin HM.2 helicopter by the end of July 2016. Looking ahead, work has already commenced to further evolve and upgrade the Royal Navy's Merlin HM.2 fleet, embellishing it with an aircraft tracker capability. With the UK's first aircraft carrier (HMS *Queen Elizabeth*) scheduled to commence sea trials during mid-2017, the Ministry of Defence announced on 16 January 2017 that £269 million had been set aside to fund the Crowsnest programme. This will provide the Royal Navy with a future maritime Intelligence Surveillance, Targeting Acquisition and Reconnaissance (ISTAR) capability. The contract will see all thirty Merlin HM.2s in service modified and 'Fit to Receive' the Crowsnest role kit, of which ten will be delivered for use throughout the fleet. For the past fifteen years, the responsibility for Airborne Surveillance and Control (ASaC) has fallen on the Royal Navy's unique fleet of Sea King Airborne Surveillance and Control Mk 7 helicopters (SKASaC), currently serving with 849 NAS based at Royal Naval Air Station Culdrose in Cornwall. These aircraft are currently scheduled to be withdrawn from service during late 2018, to be replaced by the Merlin HM.2 mounted system. Crowsnest is an integral part of the Carrier Enabled Power Projection (CEPP) capability, which will deliver two Queen Elizabeth Class aircraft carriers and the Lockheed Martin F-35B Lightning II to operate from their decks, alongside other maritime and battlefield rotary assets. By mid-2020, the Royal Navy's current fleet of thirty Merlin HM.2s based at Culdrose will have two primary roles; Anti-Submarine Warfare (ASW) and ASAC incorporating Airborne Early Warning, ISTAR and Command and Control (C2).

The Merlin HM.2 will continue to provide the Royal Navy with a truly world-class platform for the next twenty years, up to and beyond its notional Out of Service Date of 2029.

Italy

With the Royal Navy ordering forty-four aircraft, the Italian government announced an order for their Marina Militare (navy) in 1997. An order of thirty-six was first envisaged but this number was cut to sixteen due to financial constraints. The order was left open with an option to purchase more if required. With EH101 production set up in Cascina Costa, the maiden flight of the first Italian EH101 (MM.81480) took place on 4 October 1999, with deliveries completed by 2006.

The navy order comprised four different versions of the EH101. The first was the Mk 110, which operated in an anti-surface warfare (ASuW) and anti-submarine warfare (ASW) role hosting a configuration similar to the British Merlin HM.1. However, the avionics suite used a number of Italian-made systems, such as the Eliradar AN/APS-784 radar, the Alenia AN/AYK-204 processor, an Alenia ECM suite and the dipping sonar would be a Honeywell HELRAS Mod 2.

The Mk 112 was configured for the airborne early warning (AEW) role. These aircraft carried the Eliradar HEW-784 radar, which is similar to the AN/APS-784 but has a larger antenna.

The Mk 410 was in a standard utility transport set-up and the Mk 413 ASH (Assault Support Helicopter) was designed as a medium/heavy multi-role platform capable of performing multiple missions: special operations, amphibious support and Search and Rescue (SAR).

These EH101s were built in Italy with the final order increasing to twenty-two helicopters. The Italian production line closed in 2007, making way for the AW139. The final two aircraft from this order were built in the UK.

Italian Navy EH101 Mk 112. (Photo: Leonardo Helicopters)

G-17-022/2-23 for the Italian Navy during a test flight in Yeovil on 3 November 2009. The AW101 production line in Italy had closed around 2007.

Royal Air Force (RAF) Merlin HC.3/3A

The RAF ordered twenty-two EH101 helicopters in March 1995, when the government gave approval to order a mixed procurement of Chinook and EH101. The most obvious difference between the RAF HC.3 and the RN HM.1 order was the rear cargo ramp, followed by the less visible but just as noticeable lack of foldable rotors, which were not required. It also differs from the Royal Navy version by having double-wheel main landing gear, whereas the RN version only has a single wheel on each of the main gears. An engine inlet particle separator system provides protection in sandy environments. High flotation tyres and efficient landing gear permit operation from soft or rough terrain. The first roll-out of the HC.3 took place in a formal ceremony at Westland's on 25 November 1998.

No. 28 (AC) Squadron reformed in 2001 at RAF Benson to operate the first Merlin HC.3 helicopters. On achieving Initial Operating Capacity (IOC), the first operational deployment commenced immediately with the squadron deploying two aircraft to Bosnia in support of the NATO-led Stabilisation Force in Bosnia and Herzegovina (SFOR), based in Banja Luka. Following this, the squadron supported many operations worldwide, including Operation TELIC in Iraq until 2009, working alongside 78 Squadron crews as the Merlin Force. Following the drawdown from Iraq operations, the Merlin Force swiftly trained aircrew and modified the aircraft to cope with higher altitudes. The squadron then deployed to Afghanistan in support of Operation HERRICK in November 2009 as 1419 Flight. The squadron formally handed over Merlin helicopter operations to 845 Naval Air Squadron on 9 July 2015 at RAF Benson and changed role to become the combined Puma and Chinook Operational Conversion Unit.

From Benson to Bastion – RAF Merlins spent four years in Afghanistan. The crew of this HC.3 are taking part in a work-up training exercise on Salisbury Plain, 19 February 2012.

Taken in lovely winter light, this is a delightful angle on this Merlin HC.3 about to land on a forward refuel point on Salisbury Plain. (Photo: Jon Coombs)

RAF Merlin HC.3 ZJ130 troop training on a foggy Salisbury Plain, 20 December 2007.

In November 2005, Merlin ZJ124/H was displayed at the Dubai Air Show, its first public appearance in that region. The aircraft was self-ferried to Dubai from RAF Benson. The journey of over 4,000 miles was flown by a single crew in just over three days. (Photo: Leonardo Helicopters)

78 Squadron re-formed in late 2008 after the RAF acquired six additional HC.3A aircraft from Denmark. It was judged that expanding 28 Squadron would not be a viable solution, thus gaining the Merlin Force its second squadron. The HC.3A differs significantly from the slightly older HC.3, most noticeably with the distinctive nose housing a weather radar and low-level IR ground avoidance system (disabled in RAF use), but also with a different cabin and window layout, closer in design to the Canadian Cormorant SAR version. The HC.3A has never seen front line service, but acted as a training aircraft, freeing more HC.3s for deployment. With the removal of UK assets operating in Afghanistan, the RAF Merlins returned home in 2014.

During a re-structure of UK assets, it was decided the RAF Merlin HC.3/3A would replace the retiring Royal Navy Sea King HC.4 (*see Chapter 10*).

78 Squadron disbanded in September 2014 when 846 NAS stood up. The Merlin helicopters were formally handed to the Royal Navy Commando Helicopter Force. Personnel from 846 NAS normally based at RNAS Yeovilton spent three years at RAF Benson in Oxfordshire to be trained by RAF instructors, who were later joined by 845 NAS. In March 2015, the first six aircraft departed RAF Benson with 846 NAS returning to RNAS Yeovilton. 845 NAS departed RAF Benson in summer 2016, taking all remaining Merlin helicopters with them, ready to start a new chapter operating with the Royal Navy.

Originally delivered to Denmark as a Mk 512, this Merlin ZJ995 was converted to HC3A standard to cover a shortfall in RAF capabilities.

Merlin HC.3A operating on a mission rehearsal exercise on Salisbury Plain, 5 February 2010.

A HC3A seen with a rarely fitted refuelling probe, 8 April 2010.

On 13 February 2008, a Merlin HC.3 carried out the first-ever air-to-air refuelling by a British helicopter when it took on fuel from an Italian Air Force C-130J tanker. (Photo: Leonardo Helicopters)

Aside from active service, during 2008, the Merlin HC.3 was certified for air to air refueling (AAR), with a flight test campaign starting on 12 February. The HC.3 supplied by the RAF flew with an AgustaWestland test crew, with air refueling provided by an Italian KC-130J Hercules air tanker. During the tests, the Merlin made both 'dry' and 'wet' contacts from both the right and left hose of the tanker, while carrying different payloads and at altitudes from 4,000 to 5,000 ft (1,220 m to 1,524 m)

Although the RAF don't use the HC.3 in an AAR capacity, these tests were fundamental for AgustaWestland to pursue future export contracts for a Combat Search and Rescue helicopter (CSAR). The Italian Air Force, along with the US, set a firm requirement of AAR capability for any potential new CSAR helicopter.

Canada

Following interest from the UK and Italy, the Canadian government placed an order in 1987 for forty-eight EH101s to replace the Royal Canadian Air Force's (RCAF) Sikorsky CH-124 Sea Kings and Boeing Vertol CH-113 Labradors. These were to be assembled in Canada under the designations CH-148 Petrel and CH-149 Chimo, operating in the anti-submarine warfare and air-sea rescue roles respectively. A change in government in 1993 saw these plans scrapped as the replacement program was cancelled.

In 1998, with the deteriorating condition of the Canadian helicopter fleet, the government announced that the Labradors would be replaced by a scaled-down Search and Rescue (SAR) variant of the EH101, carrying the designation CH-149 Cormorant. Unlike the first cancelled contract, these fifteen aircraft were to be built entirely in Italy.

The maiden flight of a Canadian CH-149 Cormorant took place at Cascina Costa on 31 May 2000. The first two CH-149s were handed over to the RCAF in a ceremony in Italy on 29 September 2001. Flown by a Canadian flight crew, these aircraft were ferried directly from Italy to Canada, via a number of crew rest and fuel stops. A RCAF CC-130 Hercules joined the helicopters at Aberdeen airport in Scotland. This aircraft provided support to

A CH-149 Cormorant takes off from a confined area in Cloud Lake, Nova Scotia, during a training flight on 8 January 2016. (Photo: RCAF)

the Cormorants as they flew over the Atlantic Ocean water legs via Iceland and Greenland. The two helicopters arrived in CFB Comox, Canada, in the second week of October 2001.

The CH-149 Cormorant had many of the features developed for the British and Italian aircraft and had been specifically configured for search and rescue operations in hazardous environments, making it ideal for Canada's challenging geography and climate. Its ice protection system allows it to operate in continuous icing conditions and its ability to withstand high winds is optimal for conducting search and rescue missions over the rough Atlantic Ocean. With its modern design techniques and advanced technology, the Cormorant was the most capable long-range search and rescue helicopter available when it entered service in 2001.

When sufficient CH-149s had been delivered, an Operational Training Unit was set up with five Cormorants at CFB Comox with 19 Wing. In service, the CH-149 was located strategically across Canada to operate with 103 Squadron, 9 Wing, Gander; 412 Squadron, 14 Wing, Greenwood; and 424 Squadron, 8 Wing, Trenton. During 2005, 424 Squadron was re-equipped with the Bell CH-146 Griffon to replace its fleet of CH-149 Cormorants as a primary SAR helicopter for central Canada.

CH-149 Cormorant helicopters sit on the tarmac at Sydney Airport, Nova Scotia, 12 March 2009. (Photo: RCAF)

CH-149 Cormorant 149907 of 442 Squadron brings a little splash of colour to a chilly December day at Vancouver International, British Columbia, Canada, on 30 December 2010. (Photo: Mark Munzel)

Two CH-149 Cormorant helicopters sit at Summerside Airport, on Prince Edward Island, during a boat camp exercise on 13 June 2015. (Photo: RCAF)

At the end of May 2017, it was confirmed by Leonardo Helicopters that 'Team Cormorant' would be re-established to execute the Cormorant Mid-Life Upgrade (CMLU) and conversion programme, extending the Cormorant to at least 2040. The project will incorporate the latest avionics, mission systems and ice protection components, as well as enhancing SAR capabilities by fitting advanced radars, sensors, tracking systems and vision enhancement equipment. This programme will also combine the current fleet of fourteen Cormorants with the additional helicopters obtained by the Canadian government following the US VH-71 presidential helicopter programme, which are currently in storage. The results from the CMLU and conversion program will not only expand the service of three SAR bases to four, but offers significant reduction in ownership costs. This whole project will be achieved without reducing the current SAR aircraft availability.

Notably, the Canadian fleet has clocked up more flight hours than any other AW101 fleet in the world, delivering essential life-saving missions to Canadians in distress. This latest announcement will see this service is continued and cost effective into the future.

Denmark

In 2001, Denmark announced the selection of the multi-role EH101 to meet its SAR and troop transport requirements following a straight competition between the Sikorsky S-92 and NH Industries NH90 to replace its long-serving fleet of Sikorsky S-61s.

In December 2001, the Danish Ministry of Defence ordered fourteen Merlins. Eight would be equipped for SAR and six for tactical troop transport. The six transport helicopters were transferred to the British Royal Air Force during 2007 to cover a shortfall in aircraft. An additional six aircraft were ordered by the UK Ministry of Defence to replace these.

As part of the NATO-led coalition in Afghanistan, Denmark sent two Merlins out to Helmand Province. These required a few modifications, including installation of door guns and electronic warfare systems. During their work-up training for Afghanistan, two Danish Merlin helicopters took part in Exercise Pashtun Jaguar, a training exercise located on the Salisbury Plain Training Area in Wiltshire, which was used to test British troops prior to deployment.

Left: ZJ993, an EH101 Mk 512 for Denmark, on a test flight, 8 February 2005.

Below: A Danish EH101 banks hard during a training exercise in the Welsh Mountain Flying Training Area. (Photo: David Ellins)

The Danish Air Force making use of the great weather and vast ranges in California. (Photo: Joe Copalman)

EH101 Mk 512, on a test flight at Westland on 17 December 2009. This final helicopter for the RDAF was delivered on 20 January 2010.

Instrumentation panels inside the Danish Mk 512. (Photo: Ian Harding)

A Danish Air Force Mk 512 with high-visibility markings from the Esk 722 Helikopter Wing, seen here on a winch training exercise. (Photo: Leonardo Helicopters)

Japan

The first commercial example of an EH101 'CIV02', JA01MP was a Series 510 version for the Tokyo Police in 1998/99, chosen primarily for its long range, high capacity and safety, essential attributes for assisting in emergency evacuations. The Merlin also gives the capability to undertake the 622-mile (1,000 km) flight to the Ogasawara Islands non-stop. The EH101's rear ramp and large passenger capacity make it ideal to extract both able-bodied and wheelchair-bound civilians that need to be evacuated quickly due to threats from natural disasters.

During 2003, AgustaWestland and Kawasaki Heavy Industries (KHI) signed a licence and purchase agreement to produce and support fourteen Japanese MCH101s. KHI had established manufacturing, test flight and support facilities at its Gifu works in Japan to support the order.

The fourteen utility rear-ramped variants of the EH101 had been selected to replace the JMSDF's fleet of Sikorsky MH-53Es and S-61s in the airborne mine countermeasures and Antarctic support roles respectively. The first Merlin G-17-518 was built by Westland's in the UK. It first flew on 15 December 2005 and was later shipped to Japan for further fitting out. The remaining helicopters were built under licence in by Kawasaki Aerospace at Gifu, in Japan.

This lovely looking EH101 has operated with the Tokyo Metropolitan Police department since 1999. It is named 'OOZORA 1'; in Japanese this means 'BIG-SKY 1'. (Photo: Leonardo Helicopters)

A KHI MCH-101, used by the JMSDF. (Photo: Leonardo Helicopters)

KHI Merlin CH-101, with 'rotors running' at the Gifu factory in Japan. (Photo: Leonardo Helicopters)

This is the first CH-101. The CH-101s are used to support Japan's Antarctic research activities. (Photo: Leonardo Helicopters)

CHAPTER SIX

Searching Far and Wide
'So That Others Might Live'

Text in this chapter is copyright and reproduced with the kind permission of Ian Harding.

Shortly after the Danish Air Force order of EH101s, the Portuguese government formally announced a decision during December 2001 to acquire twelve Merlins for Search and Rescue (SAR), combat SAR and Fishery Protection.

On 22 December 2004, the first aircraft was delivered to Portugal, flying directly from the AgustaWestland (AW) factory at Vergiate, Italy, to its new home at Montijo air base near Lisbon to operate with 751 Squadron 'Pumas'. Just over twelve months later in February 2006, the process of transition from the Puma to the Merlin got underway in earnest when the Merlin replaced the Puma in the SAR role at Montijo.

A close look at any map quickly confirms that Portugal is in a commanding position looking out on the formidable Atlantic Ocean. As far as SAR and medical evacuation (Medevac) are concerned, statistics alone will never truly reflect the scale and size of the

'Searching far and wide' – 751 Squadron. (Photo: Jorge Ruivo)

'The Boss' of 751 Squadron 2011–17, commanding officer Lieutenant Colonel João Carita, starts engine number one during a test flight. November 2016.

maritime patrol task faced by the Força Aérea Portuguesa (Portuguese Air Force, PrtAF) which is made more complex by its islands, Madeira and the Azores, located 535 miles (861 km) and 930 miles (1,500 km) from Lisbon respectively. Despite Portugal's mainland being of a relatively small size, Portugal's maritime patrol area is one of the largest in the world. With this in mind, the choice of helicopter to ultimately succeed its fleet of upgraded and aging Aerospatiale SA-330S Puma helicopters was always going to be an important one. Being able to bridge the gap between Lisbon and the Azores, something the Puma could not do easily, was a vital consideration in the evaluation process, which ultimately saw the selection of the AgustaWestland EH101 Merlin over its main competitors, the Sikorsky S-92 and Eurocopter AS-532 Cougar Mk 2.

The PtrAF acquired three different variants, which were the EH101 Mk 514 used for SAR, the EH101 Mk 515 used for Fishery Protection (SIFICAP) and the EH101 Mk 516 used for Combat Search and Rescue (CSAR).

To ensure that Portugal's Alert SAR duty would not suffer during the transition from Puma to Merlin, the PrtAF had to use the same aircrew. When the first five aircrews were trained and established on the Merlin, the SAR alert at Montijo changed from Puma to Merlin, although the ageing Puma continued to provide coverage on the islands of Madeira and Azores. The Madeira detachment became the first island to convert to the Merlin when eight complete aircrew were fully operational. As the tenth crew stood up, the Azores detachment then became solely Merlin-equipped too.

Any issues during the introduction of the Merlin were supported by the Puma throughout the gradual transition. The order for the Portuguese complement of twelve

An EH101 Mk 514 SAR of the Portuguese Air Force taxiies for a test flight. November 2016.

EH101s was completed with the arrival of the final Merlin at BA6 Montijo in July 2006. At this point, operational plans for the Merlin were proceeding well and, having received its full complement of aircraft, it was no surprise the decision was taken by the PrtAF on 30 November 2006 to retire the last of its Puma aircraft, stationed at BA4 Lajes air base in the Azores. Three Merlins from 751 Squadron began operations the very next day. Unfortunately, this transition did not go as smoothly as was hoped. During the next few months, as a result of a mixture of maintenance problems and a shortage of manufacturer spare parts, it became clear that action was required to ensure that the SAR mission to the Azores was not compromised. With initial operational serviceability levels on the detached Merlins proving to be lower than expected, the decision was taken during late 2007/early 2008 to reactivate 752 Squadron, which was the original Puma squadron in the Azores from 1978 to 1993, and reintroduce the Puma fleet to complement the Merlin in long-range SAR in the Azores. Although a considerable disappointment, this decision was necessary in order to maintain the PrtAF mission, which provides a vital lifeline for the people of the islands that comprise the Azores archipelago.

Quite clearly, these initial issues were not acceptable either for the PrtAF or AW, who announced in August 2008 that a contract had been signed with Locação de Equipamentos de Defesa SA (DEFLOC) through its newly formed subsidiary company, AW Portugal, to provide long term support to the PrtAF fleet of twelve Merlin helicopters. Similar to the Integrated Merlin Operational Support (IMOS) agreement in place with the Royal Air Force and Royal Navy, this Full In Service Support (FISS) contract saw AW take full responsibility for the second-level maintenance of the aircraft as well as the provision of spares, repairs and technical support services for a total of fifteen years divided into three five-year segments. With staff from AW working alongside those from other local companies, which included OGMA (Oficina Geral de Material Aéronautico) and Indústria Aeronáutica de Portugal, S.A since the start of 2009, the short-term aim of this initiative was simply to resolve all issues and improve the serviceability record of the aircraft as soon as possible.

While these issues provided an inauspicious start for the striking green and brown camouflaged PrtAF Merlin fleet, there is no doubting the subsequent ability of their aircraft to excel in all three of its designated roles.

19605 departs from
the helipad at Montijo.
November 2016.

All twelve aircraft, delivered to three different specifications, are capable of undertaking SAR, Medevac and tactical transport. As previously mentioned, specific variants have been configured differently to enable them to undertake specialist CSAR and Fisheries Protection. The main difference with the Fisheries Protection variant is that it is equipped with a cabin mission console for operating the 360 degree scan radar, a specific mission management computer and software linked to a digital camera, video recording and stabilised binoculars, which are controlled by a Electromagnetic Intelligence (ELINT) Navigator who operates the FLIR and maintains secure communications with the Fisheries Department in Lisbon, who request the mission. Once the request has been made by the Department, mission responsibility passes to PrtAF Operational Command, who controls the mission in 'real-time'. Taking a closer look at the CSAR-equipped aircraft in particular makes you appreciate just how capable and impressive this aircraft is aside from its 'standard' features. As one might expect, the CSAR aircraft contain a comprehensive Defensive Aids Suite (DAS), which includes an integrated self-protection system plus Radar Warning Receivers (RWR), a Missile Warning System (MWS), a Counter Measures Dispensing System (CMDS), which includes chaff and flare dispensers, together with some classified equipment for secure communications, reinforced crew seating able to withstand the PrtAF specified crash loadings and other tactical use devices such as a Personnel Locator System. They are additionally equipped with folding tail and main rotor systems enabling them to embark and operate from naval frigates.

In terms of comparing raw power and performance, the Merlin has this in abundance with three Rolls-Royce Turbomeca RTM322 turbo-shaft engines, rated at 1,567 KW compared with two Turbomeca Makila engines rated at 1,400 KW for the older modified Puma the Merlin replaced. With three engines, auxiliary power units and generators linked to each engine, which are further cross-linked (in the event of an engine loss or failure, cross-linked generators will generate power from the remaining two engines and distribute it appropriately), the aircraft has the kind of fail-safe security needed during over-water SAR, especially when potentially operating alone at an extended range. Further, if the main systems were to fail in flight or electrical power is lost for any reason various

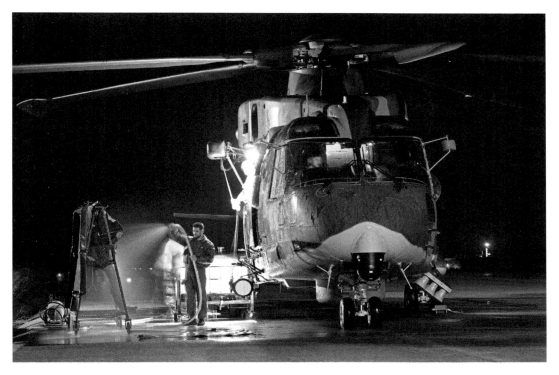

A fresh water hose-down after a night training exercise off the coast of Lisbon. Sea water is a highly corrosive substance so the hosing down of the AW101 helps protect the life of the components on the helicopter.

back-up systems sequentially 'kick-in' to maintain flight critical systems even if this means losing cockpit electronic display systems, although that is a worst-case situation. The safety approach of the EH101 (now AW101) management systems are broadly speaking to retain the mission if possible and, if not, maintain flight or ultimately provide a survivable ditching capability. Emergency floatation equipment operates automatically should the aircraft ditch for any reason. Common to all PrtAF variants are two search and rescue hoists; a primary hydraulic hoist and a secondary electrical hoist, which would be used as a back-up (weight limits on each are 272 kg and 136 kg respectively), belly-mounted 360 degree SELEX Galileo Avionica APS-717 Search Radar, which is able to identify and monitor thirty-two surface targets simultaneously, night vision goggles (NVG) capability enabling day/night operations, extremely powerful NITESUN searchlight for night operations and Forward Looking Infrared Radar (FLIR) and other multi-mission systems, which include Global Positioning System (GPS) and Inertial Navigation System (INS) as well as conventional radio navigation aids and direction-finding receptors.

Comparing the difference between the Merlin and Puma is actually quite easy and can be looked at from two points of view. In terms of raw performance, the aircraft upgrade basically translates to a factor of two. Twice the internal payload (around 4 tonnes), twice the range (850 nautical miles (NM)) and radius of action (400 NM), twice the passengers (thirty-five seated troops at standard combined weight of 264 lbs (120kgs); or

Up close and personal just before engine start at Montijo during November 2016.

A Portuguese Air Force EH101 warming engines before a night training exercises with the Portuguese Navy in the waters around Lisbon, November 2016.

casualties (sixteen stretchers). As for capabilities, the difference is even greater. To begin with the Merlin has advanced avionics, which include a four-axis auto-pilot including advanced modes, capable of transitioning-up, navigating, performing search patterns and transitioning down to coupled hover in autopilot. This not only frees up the flight crew for mission management, it also means the aircraft can hover more safely over water at night, which is essential for SAR. The Puma could not do this. The plethora of integrated systems includes a 360 degree search radar electro-optics turret that contains the most recent thermal imaging technology and substantially enhances mission performance.

For all the Merlin's advanced technical features, one of the most impressive is its range capability, which is certainly being put to the test by the PrtAF.

The journey to Madeira or the Azores is quite routinely done as the PrtAF rotate crews every fifteen days. The stretch from the mainland to Madeira over water is over 500 NM and the Azores are a further 620 NM. Ferrying from Montijo to Lajes in the Azores takes around 10 hours of flight time plus an intermediate thirty to sixty-minute rest stop for refuelling at Porto Santo. This was achievable in the Puma, which had about the same cruise speed (120 knots), but considering its lower endurance, the PrtAF spent many years doing that route on very tight fuel calculations. To make things worse, the notoriously severe Azorean Atlantic weather was always a major factor and generally a very negative one. The PrtAF always had to consider any strong en-route winds against the slow cruising speeds. The impact of strong winds on a journey could be huge. If necessary, the aircraft would be taken apart and the journey made in the back of a Hercules. Nowadays, with the Merlin and its huge fuel capacity, two-engine cruise capability and full auto-pilot, it is a far simpler task. Now when the PrtAF are called into action, they can now spend up to 7 hours on station or complete missions some 400 NM (740 km) from base and return when fitted with long-range fuel tanks.

The motto of 751 Squadron 'Pumas', '*Para Que Outros Vivam*', which translates to 'So that others may live', succinctly defines their primary role. As you enter their pristine squadron facilities at Montijo, the entrance notice board confirming the number of lives saved to date (3,627 up to April 2017) leaves visitors in no doubt as to the importance of this squadron's role within Portugal's extensive maritime zone. The Portuguese Merlin has flown 22,830 flying hours up to the same date. SAR operations are always visible and high profile yet those directly involved always maintain a humble disposition. Operating so far away from base and out to sea represents a huge personal challenge let alone one for the aircraft. It is therefore imperative that knowledge of the job and technology work in perfect unison as far as circumstances allow. To say their work is varied is an understatement and frankly it is impossible to truly appreciate how difficult some of the situations these crews find themselves in are.

Fantastic photo showing the brown and green scheme on this Combat Search and Rescue (CSAR) EH101-516. (Photo: PrtAF)

CHAPTER SEVEN

The American Dream

On 23 July 2002, Lockheed Martin and AW announced that they had signed a ten-year agreement to jointly market, manufacture and support the EH101 in the United States. It would be designated as the US101, an American version of the Merlin with 64 per cent of the helicopter manufactured in America. The aim was to exploit the aircraft in

What could have been! CGI of the US101 fleet proposed to the United States. (Photo: Leonardo Helicopters)

three major roles: US Air Force Combat Search and Rescue, US Coast Guard Search and Rescue and US Marine Corps Executive/ Presidential Transport. 'Team US101' was led by Lockheed Martin Systems Integration, a subsidiary of Lockheed Martin, which served as the prime contractor and systems operator. AW provided the aircraft design and specifications for Bell Helicopter, headquartered in Fort Worth, Texas, to produce the aircraft in the United States under licence.

On 15 May 2003, AW signed an agreement with Bell Helicopter, who would undertake final assembly of the US101 in the USA. AW would manufacture the main rotor blades and main fuselage sections at its Yeovil plant while other components, including the gearbox, were produced at Cascina Costa, Italy. This represented a 36 per cent work share. The remaining 64 per cent was split between Lockheed Martin and Bell Helicopter. The US101 project included large upgrades to the previous AW101, incorporating the installation of the up-rated General Electric CT7-8E engines and new advanced BERP IV rotor blades.

The EH101 510 series prototype, under its UK B conditions registration G-17-510, was the airframe used to conduct the initial assessments and after early initial flights at Yeovil, the majority of the CT7-8E engine programme was conducted at SCLA, Victorville, California. These were more powerful than just an executive transport helicopter. It was to be 2,500 hp (1.865 kW) engines, which would provide approximately a 12 per cent increase in power over the earlier CT7 family of engines. This increased the payload capabilities of the helicopter by 2,000 lbs (907 kg) when operating in hot and high environments.

RAF Merlin from No. 28 (AC) Squadron flying over the Statue of Liberty in New York while on a United States sales tour. (Photo: Leonardo Helicopters)

Back in February 2002, the US Marine Corps had conducted a study to identify potential replacement rotorcraft for the ageing Sikorsky VH-3D Presidential Transport helicopters, famously referred to as 'Marine One' in their primary role. On 18 December 2003, the United States Department of Defence (DOD) issued a request for proposals for the supply of twenty-three helicopters to be used as a replacement for the eleven VH-3Ds and eight VH-60Ns of the Marine Corps' HMX-1 squadron. AgustaWestland with the US101 and Sikorsky aircraft with the VH-92 responded to the request and entered competitive bids.

On 28 January 2005, the DOD announced that the joint team of Lockheed Martin and AW had secured the contract for the new Presidential helicopter, known at that time as VXX. An initial order for four test vehicles (TV) and five pilot production (P-P) aircraft was awarded after an extensive evaluation of available solutions. The US101 was thereafter re-designated as the VH-71 Kestrel.

The VH-71 was perceived as a Command and Control platform that would provide the President of the United States (POTUS) with seamless communications connectivity at all times and fulfil the historic 'Marine One' mission requirements. Due to the tight development schedule, it was decided to lease an initial aircraft to commence flight and maintenance training. To meet the timetable TV1, which was an Italian Navy EH101, arrived at Patuxent River on 2 November 2005. The first actual VH-71 Kestrel (TV2) made its maiden flight at the AW facility in Yeovil on 3 July 2007. Despite being built under contract to the US Navy, this aircraft was assembled and prepared in the UK for its first-flight. During the forty-minute check-flight, AgustaWestland Chief Test-Pilot Don Maclaine and Senior Test-Pilot Dick Trueman performed general aircraft handling checks, tested flight characteristics at varying speeds up to 135 knots, and evaluated the on-board avionics systems functions. The US Navy-owned test vehicles TV-2 and TV-5 arrived at NAS Patuxent River in November and

G-17-510, in US101 markings, flies over Yeovil. (Photo: Leonardo Helicopters)

G-17-510, in US101 markings, showing off a set of BERP IV rotor blades. (Photo: Leonardo Helicopters)

December 2007 respectively aboard a US Air Force C-17 military transport flown from RNAS Yeovilton, nearby to AgustaWestland's Yeovil manufacturing-base. TV2 and TV5 were primarily tasked with structural/propulsion testing and pilot-training.

During 2008, TV3 and TV4 arrived at Lockheed Martin Systems Integration in Owego, New York, for mission systems integration. Following this they joined TV1, TV2 and TV5 at Patuxent River for testing of the avionics and mission systems. The first production VH-71A, Pilot-Production 1 (P-P1), made its maiden flight on 22 September 2008 from Yeovil. In October 2008, John Young, the US Under-Secretary of Defence for Acquisition, Technology and Logistics stated that the VH71 project was very high on a list of potential cuts following changes in the government. Shortly after President Obama took office in 2009 the decision was made to cancel the VH71 project. On 15 May 2009, Ashton B. Carter, who succeeded the Bush-appointed John Young in the role, issued an Acquisition Decision Memorandum directing that the VH-71 program be cancelled. This was primarily due to cost overruns, largely due to the extensive upward-specification of the product, allied to political pressure from America.

This anecdote serves as an example of the chaotic process: mid-programme the Navy said, 'We need this bird to have a built-in ladder, so we can do maintenance wherever the helicopter is without external support equipment.' AW said, 'Yes, we have an off-the-shelf version of the airframe that has a built-in ladder.' Then the White House came back and said, 'That ladder is on the right side, and it will be seen in all the pictures of the President getting in and out of the helicopter. We want it on the left side.' AW said, 'We don't have an off-the-shelf helicopter with the ladder on the left side, but we can build a custom version.' Then the Navy came back and said, 'According to Navy standards, each rung has to hold a 200-pound mechanic plus parts.' This forced AW to upgrade the internal structure. The added weight dictated further modifications to meet the original performance specifications and those changes required other changes. The cost and delay spiral continued.

The first test VH-71A, test vehicle TV2, made its initial flight on 3 July 2007 at AgustaWestland's facility in Yeovil.

Pilot Production 1 takes first flight at Westland's. (Photo: Leonardo Helicopters)

The VXX Project was terminated in February 2009 amid published costs of $13 billion and at the personal behest of President Obama.

On 1 June 2009, the US Navy announced that the contract was officially cancelled and that remaining funds were to be redirected into upgrades of the existing fleet of VH-3D and VH-60N helicopters. The Congressional Research Service (CRS) examined the financial implications of the President's plan and discovered that axing the VH-71 and retrofitting the VH-3D would, in the long run, end up costing the US taxpayers somewhere in the range of $14–21 billion, not including the $3 billion they'd already spent on the Kestrel R&D so far. A savings bonanza, it definitely was not! Plus any future fleet purchases wouldn't be affordable until at least 2024, by which point the Sea Kings would be well past their 'sell-by' date. The CRS tendered a four-option proposal for continuing with a variation of the existing Kestrel programme. Firstly, continue the Kestrel model as currently developed using Increment I and II versions as progressive prototypes. This option would have cost an estimated $10 billion and seen the helicopters in the air by 2019. Secondly, build twenty-three units of just the Increment I Kestrel, which would have cost an estimated $6.4 billion and seen them ready by 2012. Thirdly, build just nineteen Increment I types for $5.9 billion with a scheduled completion date of late 2012. Finally, spend just $1.4 billion to upgrade the existing Sea King fleet, accepting that plan would not actually satisfy any of the requirements for future presidential helicopters and would still require total replacement in the short-term.

Even in the face of what was considered such compelling financial logic, all the options were rejected and the Kestrels were consigned to storage and history in one stroke. This lends some credence to the thought by some that the mere thought of the President of the United States flying in a European-designed and developed helicopter was too much to bear!

Nine VH-71s had been completed by the time of the cancellation. Subsequently, in early 2011 these nine VH-71s, several bespoke outfitted, were purchased by Canada for the bargain price of $164 million including delivery, which is less than £12 million each at historic currency rates. The VH-71 aircraft had been mothballed for two years at NAS Patuxent and were delivered to Canada for spare parts recovery to maintain the fleet of heavily used AgustaWestland CH-149 Cormorant Search and Rescue helicopters, although other options were investigated.

There are several types of contract cancellation, but generally it involves financial penalties to be borne by the cancelling party, which invariably results in compensation, in this case to AW. Despite the cancellation of the project, the AW101 development itself benefited positively from the aborted process, an example being the subsequent fleet-wide adoption of the higher performance General Electric CT7-8E engine first fitted to the VH-71.

CHAPTER EIGHT

AW101 in the Limelight

The AW101 shot to stardom in 2012 when it appeared in the opening ceremony of the Olympic Games and then, later in the year, the James Bond blockbuster film *Skyfall*.

During the London Olympic Games in 2012, a specially painted AW101 appeared in a patriotic red, white and blue colour scheme. Taking just a weekend to complete, the helicopter was hidden away and shrouded in secrecy at the BBC *Top Gear* studio at Dunsfold Park. A team of painters working for Flying Colours sprayed the Merlin with water-soluble paint. Reaching the climax of the ceremony, the AW101 flew over the Olympic stadium, releasing 8 billion pieces of confetti on to Team GB and the 80,000-strong crowd. A special chute was adapted for the confetti drop, viewed by billions worldwide on television. After the event, the AW101 returned to Dunsfold to lose its unique one-off paint job and the helicopter was reconfigured back to its normal role.

Later that year the AW101 was once more thrust into the limelight, when it appeared in an explosive action sequence during the James Bond film *Skyfall*.

Westland Chief Test Pilot Andy Strachan flew the daredevil manoeuvres in AW101 G-17-510, which had been modified and painted to star in the movie. Filmed on Hankley Common in Surrey, the AW101 spent 15 flight hours on stage rehearsing and shooting the action scenes,

ZK001, painted in a one-off Union Jack scheme for the London Olympics Games opening ceremony, 23 July 2012. (Photo: Ian Harding)

'Some men are coming to kill us. We are going to kill them first.' *Skyfall*. (Photo: Ian Harding)

The camera helicopter and the AW101 work close together to film the action scenes. (Photo: Liam Daniels)

flying alongside a camera ship helicopter to record the sequence. The helicopter's role in the movie was transportation for the villain, Silva. The AW101 can be seen transporting Silva and his men to 'Skyfall Lodge', where Bond and M are in hiding. The scene includes a dramatic firefight, causing the house to be severely damaged.

During this clip Bond constructs a bomb that later blows up the house, damaging the helicopter with debris. In a typical movie style the helicopter crashes into the remaining building, resulting in a spectacular explosion.

Less well known is the pivotal part G-17-510 (CIV01) has played and still plays in the already aforementioned support of the AW101 development. This Mk 510 was first registered I-AGWB and first flew in Brindisi, Italy, on 17 June 1997. It was designed as the civilian demonstrator (CIV01).

Later in its career, it went onto support the US101 project. On 26 September 2006, EH101 G-17-510 (CIV01), fitted with new technology British Experimental Rotor Program (BERP) IV main rotor blades, more powerful CT7-8E engines and a new integrated cockpit display system, made its first flight at Yeovil.

'Running in hot', looking for the target. 'Always got to make an entrance.' (Photo: Ian Harding)

I-AGWH, a CIV01 later re-registered as G-17-510. (Photo: Leonardo Helicopters)

G-17-510 with camera attached on cold-weather trials. (Photo: Leonardo Helicopters)

The BERP IV program had commenced in 2000 with a technology selection and integration phase leading to the design and manufacturing phase in 2002. The thirteen-month flight test programme started in 2006, during which the AW101 was flown at speeds up to 198 knots and at altitudes of 13,000 ft. The enhancements in blade manufacturing processes were clearly demonstrated during trials flying; blade interchange ability had been further improved to the stage where little or no tracking adjustments were required when changing blades.

The BERP IV blades represent the next generation of rotor technology developed under a jointly funded AW and UK Ministry of Defence rotor technology development and demonstration programme. The blades incorporate an improved plan form, new aerofoil sections and an advanced aero elastically tailored structure to provide reduced vibration, 10 knots additional cruise speed and 1,433 lbs (650 kg) additional lift capability over the standard AW101 Merlin main rotor blades. AgustaWestland test pilot Dick Trueman said, 'The harder these blades work the better they perform; they give the AW101 a very useful improvement in lift capability. The already smooth AW101 is even smoother with these blades – vibration levels were so low we often had to check the active vibration control system on the AW101 was switched off during testing.'

G-17-510 also completed a series of icing trials, giving the aircraft the same exceptional icing clearance of the predecessor, allowing flight in known icing conditions.

Following an extensive flight test programme the CT7-8E engines were certified and proved totally reliable during all phases of testing. The new fully integrated flight and mission cockpit display system utilises five 25 cm x 20 cm (10 in. x 8 in.) LCD main displays that give AW101 pilots 70 per cent more display area, enhancing their management of flight, system and mission data. The new fully articulated tail rotor has been designed to take advantage of the extra power available from the engines and to allow the AW101 to operate at its current 34,392 lbs (15,600 kg) maximum all-up weight as well as future higher take off weights. The new tail rotor gives the same excellent control margins as the original tail rotor design but at the higher weights, including the ability to hover in 40 knot crosswinds. Recently G-17-510 has become re-registered serial AW101.

G-17-510, with faded US101 markings, lands back at Westland's after a test flight, 10 March 2010.

Re-registered from G-17-510 to AW101, 30 November 2016.

Chapter Nine

World Exports Gather Momentum

Thanks to the upgrades received during the US101 project, the AW101 became desirable to a number of overseas export customers. Already established in the Search and Rescue and military markets, AW decided to design a specialised luxury variant. The AW101 emerged as an ultimate transport for heads of state and Very, Very Important Persons (VVIP).

Algerian AW101, still in primer, on a test flight at Westland's, 18 December 2009.

Note the search light addition on this AW101-610 for Algeria. 7 April 2010.

The first AW101-610 for Algeria on a test flight at Westland's, 10 November 2010.

AW101-610 for Algeria, with national markings applied, on a test flight at Westland's, 8 April 2010.

Algeria purchased six AW101 Mk 610s in 2007, to be operated by the Algerian naval forces. This is a dedicated SAR version, with a 360 degree search radar and FLIR/EO turret under the nose.

AW101-642 of the Military Air Liaison Group (GLAM), a division of the Algerian Air Force. (Photo: Leonardo Helicopters)

AW101-640 for Saudi Arabia. Saudi Arabia acquired two for VVIP and heads of state use. (Photo: Ian Harding)

The AW101 has a cabin 30 per cent larger than its nearest competitor and it can fly up to 1,000 km, while multiple redundancy of critical systems and components gives the aircraft unmatched levels of safety and survivability.

A contract for two AW101 VVIP helicopters for Turkmenistan Airlines was signed at the Farnborough International Air Show in 2010. (Photo: Leonardo Helicopters)

India signed a contract to purchase twelve AgustaWestland AW101 helicopters in February 2010. The contract was frozen in February 2013 and the contract was eventually cancelled.

Painted in colours for a potential order to Azerbaijan, 15 July 2015.

The Nigerian Air Force operates a pair of VIP-configured AW101 Mk 641 helicopters.

Originally part of a larger order for VVIP replacements in Indonesia, it is unclear what internal configuration was fitted to this AW101 at delivery. 17 January 2017.

CHAPTER TEN

Current Front Line AW101

Italian Air Force

In 2009 the Italian Air Force made a requirement to replace their fleet of Agusta/Sikorsky HH-3 Pelican amphibious medium-lift helicopters.

The new helicopters' prerequisites included survivability, power and flexibility. The AW101 was chosen as the ideal replacement and during 2010 a contract was signed for twelve new variant HH-101A Caesar helicopters with an option of purchasing three more. The first production HH-101A made its maiden flight at AW, Yeovil, on 19 March 2014.

A number of officials from the Italian Air Force and government witnessed the flight, including the Italian Air Force Chief of Staff Gen. Pasquale Preziosa and the Italian Ambassador Domenico Terracciano.

Gen. Pasquale Preziosa said, 'The HH-101A will respond to the Italian Air Force's needs for Personnel Recovery and Special Forces Operations. It will also support SAR, MEDEVAC and Slow Mover Intercept operations which are extremely important to provide effective

HH-101 Caesar over the south coast of England on a test flight from Westland's. (Photo: Leonardo Helicopters)

Room with a view!
HH-101A of the
Italian Air Force.
(Photo: Robin Coenders)

Menacing looking
head-on shot of an
Italian Air Force
HH-101A, callsign 'Lord'.
(Photo: Niels Roman)

A M134d mounted
Gatling-type machine
gun on the back
ramp of an ITAF
HH-101A Caesar,
5 October 2015. (Photo:
Domenico Marchi)

support to the Italian community. Thanks to its performances, versatility and reliability, the HH-101A is the best solution for the Italian Air Force's future operational capability requirements.'

During 2015, military-type certification was granted and deliveries could start. The HH-101A will also be able to meet the troop transport and utility role plus feature an air-to-air refuelling kit for extended range operations. By May 2017, six HH-101As had been delivered to the Italian Air Force, all operating with the 81° Centro Addestramento SAR (81st Search and Rescue Training Centre) as part of 15° Stormo in Cervia. In the future Cervia will be the Main Operating Base for the HH-101A.

Norway – Super SAR!

Text in this chapter is copyright and reproduced with the kind permission of Ian Harding.

Many consider the AW 101 that will be delivered to Norway as the world's most advanced and capable SAR platform ever. The aircraft is known as the Norwegian All Weather Search and Rescue Helicopter or NAWSARH.

On 19 December 2013, following almost two years of competitive assessment, the Norwegian Ministry of Justice and Public Security (MJPS) announced it had awarded AW the contract for sixteen AW101 (Mk 612) helicopters (including an option for a further six

Unveiling the Royal Norwegian Air Force AW101-612 at Westland's, 31 May 2015. (Photo: Ian Harding)

aircraft) plus customised support and training for fifteen years valued at approximately £1 billion (€1.15 billion) to meet the Norwegian All Weather SAR Helicopter (NAWSARH) requirement. In service, the AW101 will replace the Royal Norwegian Air Force's (RNoAF) twelve AW Sea King Mk 43B helicopters, which have served for the last forty-four years with 330 Squadron, which is Norway's dedicated SAR and Medevac squadron. All aircraft are scheduled for delivery between 2017 and 2020 and current plans see AW101 operations at each of its six SAR bases transitioning at projected six-month intervals.

Norway's geography offers environmental challenges in providing adequate SAR facilities for its population and maritime responsibility. From north to south, Norway measures approximately 1,125 miles (1,800 km) and to ensure full coverage, 330 Squadron will eventually deploy two helicopters and personnel permanently to each base on SAR duty, and AW along with its commercial partners will be involved in the support of these aircraft from the outset. One aircraft will be available 24/7 on fifteen-minute alert while others will be in maintenance or ready to go as needed. This will be sufficient to meet Norway's stated 99 per cent aircraft availability Statement of Operating Intent (SOI) requirement.

These six bases – Banak, Bodø, Florø, Sola (Stavanger), Ørland on the Atlantic coast and Rygge on the Skaggerak coast – ensure the majority of Norway can be reached within ninety minutes' flight-time from one of the bases. To meet extended SAR call-outs the Norwegian aircrews are well-practiced in hot refuelling from any location where fuel is available, such as oil-rigs or ships. The latter includes 'in-flight' refuelling, but not conventionally as they refuel from a ship at sea using a method called Hover-In-Flight-Refuelling (HIFR). This procedure requires the aircrew to lift a fuel-line from the ship's deck using the helicopter's rescue hoist and connect it to the helicopter's pressure refuel point while remaining in the hover. It may sound complicated, but with training will become a common event.

The combination of terrain, weather and the mission profile make Norway's SAR assignment one of the toughest in the world. Small wonder then that the world's attention was captivated when Norway awarded this landmark contract to AW. The award not only reflects the trust and confidence that one of the world's great SAR nations has for AW and

A computer generated image of the Norwegian AW101 configuration.

the AW101 programme itself, but also stems from many years of successfully operating their venerable Sea Kings on fifteen-minute notice, 24/7.

Unlike the UK, Norwegian SAR is still undertaken by the RNoAF, although the contract and funding is managed and administered by the Norwegian MJPS. Their precise operational requirements, which included SAR, Fire-fighting, Environmental Protection, Missions of Public Interest and Emergency/Disaster Relief, were set out in an extremely challenging SOI. Norway has been very proud of their highly visible red and white Sea King helicopters and the service they provide, therefore the choice to continue with the same striking colour scheme on the AW101 was perhaps an easier decision.

Norway's Mk 612 design specifications have invariably advanced the AW101's evolutionary process. Their SOI incorporated a significant number of specific mission requirements in a comprehensive document detailing in-service performance, mission systems and capability, crew operating-conditions, environmental, range and payload requirements. Typical of a potential scenario is the rescue of twenty people in distress at sea at 150 nautical miles (278 km) from what they call the 'straight base-line', this being an average line drawn around the Norwegian coast, yet still be able to return to base (RTB). The ultimate capability request is for the AW101 to fly to the limit of the national boundary at around 360 nautical miles (666 km), winch up two people in an average hover time of approximately two to five minutes per person and RTB or a forward location for refuelling. Adverse weather conditions will always impact a plan and Norway can be susceptible to poor weather, which can severely hamper a direct transit. For other operational requirements like fire-fighting, the AW101 is cleared to carry fire-fighters and their equipment, which will include six or more equipment containers secured near the door to expedite deployment to a ship or a remote ground location via the hoist. Assistance with suppressing a fire on board a passenger ferry and rescue of the personnel represents yet another mission scenario Norway rehearses. Extended range, while very important to the SAR mission, will not use the 'normal' air-to-air refuelling capability via the forward probe, as utilised by the Italian Air Force in their HH-101A acquisition and optional on some Royal Navy variants. Clearly the facility could be provided, but compatible air tankers are not part of Norway's equipment at this time. The AW101's typical range is 750 nautical miles (over 1,390 km), which can be extended to 900 nautical miles (1,666 km) in SAR configuration using internal auxiliary fuel tanks. Other options for extending range include shutting down one of the three uprated GE. CT7-8 turboshaft engines and adopting the AW101 two-engine range-enhancing cruise capability and the previously noted HIFR opportunities. The Norwegian order has these later General Electric engines fitted as standard to this helicopter as a direct benefit of experience gleaned from the failed US order.

First impressions were important and computer generated images produced by AW confirmed how impressive Norway's AW101s would look. Recent photo images of the air tests show the new AW101 resplendent in a similar external paint scheme to the Norwegian Sea Kings. Each aircraft has the same prominent black nosecone used by the Danish and latest Italian Air Force AW101 variants. This will house even more equipment such as weather radar, various obstacle detection systems plus a Selex ES Active Electronically Scanned Array (AESA) radar. AW confirmed that the Norwegian SOI required a system to independently and simultaneously control two radar modes using the same solution (for example weather and search modes) to improve the flight crew's total situational awareness (SA) during missions

AW101-612 ZZ101
with the serial
0264 for Norway,
22 August 2016.

in hostile weather conditions. This system will enable flight crew to electronically beam-steer the radar to obtain radar images of the picture outside the helicopter, especially the proximity of unsighted mountains, which are then compiled with other sensor data to develop a clear image of the surrounding flying conditions. Norway's aircraft will incorporate the very latest in terrain awareness systems. These solutions will ultimately provide huge benefits for both safety and efficiency, allowing the crews to plan each phase of the mission en route in real-time. Such systems represent a huge technology leap forward from the Sea King, which will improve flight-crew confidence, especially for the Mission System Operator (MSO), whose role within the flight-crew is, amongst other specified tasks, to co-ordinate the mission routing, search profile and manage communications with external agencies.

Norway's six-person SAR crew composition is relatively unique, comprising two pilots, and MSO, a flight-engineer (who operates the hoist), a rescue swimmer (who is also a trained paramedic) and a doctor/anaesthesiologist. Five of these are military personnel, while the doctors work for the local Health Trust and are funded through them. Norway refers to its pilots and the MSO as the 'flight-crew'. In considering the avionics and mission system upgrade, it's conceivable that 'crew' duties will evolve over time to realise the full capability demonstrated by their AW101 helicopter. In terms of rear crew layout, the MSO 'booth' will be part of an adaptive console design utilised specifically for Norway. In standard configuration, the rear cabin can have up to two medical stations and six passenger seats, but this number can be significantly increased as required, depending on the nature of the mission. Rear crew seats will be on a sliding mechanism, which will enable them to move easily to quickly reconfigure the layout for the specific mission.

During rescues with the cabin door open, the flight engineer will operate the hoists while the MSO will operate the aircraft's hover trim control (HTC). This system enables the MSO, who is best placed to see the rescue scene, to manoeuvre and position the aircraft precisely within small parameters independently of the pilot's control manoeuvres. The integrated avionics and wireless communications aboard their AW101's ensure greater crew integration and cohesion during such events.

ZZ102 for Norway on an electromagnetic compatibility (EMC) test, 21 March 2017.

While cabin volume is only marginally greater than the Sea King, the 'usable' volume proved very appealing to Norway, with the AW101 having the height in-cabin to stand up throughout the whole floor area. This clearly supports high-capacity emergency relief, which is high on Norway's agenda, utilising its larger sliding door, which enhances the crew's visibility and enables rapid passenger and aircrew ingress/egress. The larger door size is also significant, for example, during a stretcher rescue as there is more room to load the stretcher into the cabin both on the ground or when airborne from either of the AW101's two hoists, one fixed, and one deployable boom hoist. Stretcher and passenger capacity is significantly greater for the AW101 and this can prove pivotal during emergency evacuations (up to fifty-four standing persons potentially). When all available internal space is utilised, the 'ramp-up' configuration can yield an additional 2.66 m³. Even with the larger capacity of the AW101, it should be noted that its overall 'footprint' is only slightly larger than that of the Sea King it replaces. For example, the location of its undercarriage coupled with its folding rotor capability means it can actually fit in to the same floor-space as a Sea King. The main rotor diameter, incorporating BERP IV blades is 18.60 m v. 18.90 m for the Sea King, which although marginally smaller are many times more efficient.

From a medical perspective, the AW101's layout provides the option of carrying and treating more than one critically ill patient in compartmentalised treatment areas as required. The stretcher layout provides sufficient room for two in-flight treatment zones complete with a full range of medical equipment and easy access. Of course, a role change could involve removing that equipment and replacing it with seats or additional fire-fighting equipment to suit the next mission requirements. Norway's AW101s are purposely adaptable to satisfy all unknown RNoAF operations as they evolve in the future.

Capacity and performance are important, but size clearly influenced Norway's acquisition of this helicopter, whose similar 'footprint' to the Sea King allows it to operate from Norway's existing Infrastructure, helipads and oil rigs without expensive modifications. Twin hoists, one at the front of the door and one at the back, are positioned exactly the same aboard the Sea King while the MSO console also follows a similar concept near the cabin door area. The inherent high ground clearance of a nominal 19 inches (50 cm) combined with rear ramp and side doors enhance Confined Area Landing (CAL) operations. Norway has a minimum ground clearance requirement, which the AW101 already met, but a primary reason for specifying a flat-panel radar system was due to concern that the radar could be damaged during a CAL in deep snow, where the risk of concealed objects is high.

Flight and SAR mission equipment

The Norwegian contract provides several areas of enhancement that are largely the result of experience gained from their challenging environment, allied to a commitment for maximising flight crew Situational Awareness (SA), Safety and Managed Workload, which is very important during long, demanding missions. The key features of the mission and avionics systems provide enhanced traffic-awareness, obstacle-detection, area-navigation and terrain-awareness/detection.

A key installation in the initial Norwegian AW101 configuration included the first application for Leonardo's Osprey MM multi-mode surveillance second-generation Active Electronically Scanned Array radar (AESA), comprising a trio of flat-panel sensors that are fitted – one in the aircraft's nose and one at the rear of each main landing gear sponsons – to provide 360 degree surveillance capability. It's also equipped with an electro-optical/ infrared sensor and automatic flight control system.

The availability of powerful eye-safe laser sources and the recent advancements in electro-optical and mechanical beam-steering components have allowed laser-based Light Detection and Ranging (LIDAR) to become a primary technology for obstacle-warning and avoidance in a variety of manned and unmanned aircraft applications. Originally known as the Laser Obstacle Avoidance Marconi (LOAM) system, presumably as a nod to its heritage, it was latterly still called 'LOAM' but with the 'M' then standing for 'Monitoring' The Selex LOAM is located in the AW101 nosecone just below the forward radar.

This system is capable of classifying the following types of obstacle:

Wires and thin obstacles such as, telephone cables, electrical cables (up to 5 mm diameter, whether electrified or not).
Trees, vertical obstacles such as posts, poles and pylons.
Structures and extended obstacles such as bridges, buildings and high ground.

The system is able to superimpose obstacle symbols over a camera or FLIR image to provide the pilot with an extraordinary display to enhance their situational awareness. LOAM can also perform 3D mapping of the terrain and present it as a wireframe overlay. If all wire detection fails there is a back-up facility of three wire-cutters angled forward, one left-side and one right-side below the forward fuselage with the third on top of the fuselage to the rear of the cockpit glazing, forward of the main rotor casing.

Avionics radars lack sufficient angular resolution to be able to detect small natural and man-made obstacles such as trees, power line cables and poles. The outstanding angular resolution and accuracy characteristics of LIDAR, coupled to its excellent detection performance in a wide range of incidence angles and weather conditions, provide an ideal solution for obstacle avoidance in low-level flying conditions. A limitation to the wider envelope of conditions is defined primarily by the available laser range performance and by the system field of view. The need for a high probability of detection is obvious since no real obstacle threat must go undetected. A low false-alarm rate is essential to limit spurious warnings that would increase the pilot's workload unnecessarily and possibly cause him to climb or turn unnecessarily. While not critical to SAR operations, such a reaction to spurious readings in military operations could result in becoming a target, requiring electromagnetic countermeasures devices.

Obstacle Proximity LiDAR System (OPLS)

Launched at Heli-Expo 2014, AW's OPLS system was designed to enhance the safety of helicopters undertaking demanding SAR and EMS roles, in particular to help aircrew avoid main and tail-rotor strikes against peripheral obstacles during low speed hovering manoeuvres in confined spaces. The system consists of three main rotor-head-mounted LiDAR (Laser imaging Detection and Ranging) sensors that generate a 360 degree radial view around the aircraft and a dedicated cockpit control panel. It ensures the fast and accurate detection and tracking of short-range obstacles up to 80 feet (25 m) away by time-of-flight measurement at different angles. Pilots can operate and monitor the system from the control panel while video and audio indications are provided on the cockpit Multi-Function Displays (MFDs) and via the aircraft's Inter-Communication System (ICS).

Increasingly becoming as important as the actual helicopter selection is the option to utilise the tailored support solutions offered by the manufacturer. During recent years especially, AW has invested heavily in a vast range of 'through life' support and training packages (including synthetic systems) at their training academies in the UK (Yeovil, Somerset), Italy (Sesto Calende), USA (Philadelphia) and Malaysia (Kuala Lumpur).

This investment includes extending its main training facilities in Italy at Sesto Calende, which has the potential for nine full flight simulators covering its full helicopter range, plus rear-crew trainers. These solutions, which are tailored to meet customer needs, range from the relatively simple provision of spares, through to crew training and ultimately to a programme considered to be fully integrated 'turn-key' support. Introducing new technology creates its own challenges, for example how to manage composites, building one's own expertise into mission systems, creating self-maintenance facilities and more, leading to customers now increasingly recognising they need more support, rather than less, especially during the initial transitional phase.

It is not a straightforward task to jump from a forty-year-old Sea King straight into a next generation AW101 and for this reason, Norway and AW have agreed on an initial fifteen-year support package, during which time Norway should have developed the infrastructure to complete much of this work themselves.

In many respects, the support package in place for Norway will be similar to the long-term (twenty-five years) Integrated Merlin Operational Support (IMOS) contract AW have in place which covers the RN Merlin variants. This type of contract is considered the best way to reduce in-service costs during the life of the platform and it also transfers the support risk (such as spares supply, sustainment, technical advice, aircraft issues) from the customer (Norwegian MJPS and RNoAF) to AW in a managed arrangement, allowing Norway to focus directly on operational effectiveness. It's an integrated support solution in forming a partnership with what AW refer to as a JAMMO (Joint Aircraft Availability Management Office), being the Norwegian Defence Logistics Organisation, and industry partners including some of the AW suppliers based in Norway.

This organisation will support them to actively manage the fleet, including maintenance planning, and also by providing an AW deployable team based in-country to ensure Norway's 99 per cent availability SOI criteria is achieved.

The selected Leonardo-Finmeccanica Osprey multi-mode (MM) surveillance radar provides second generation Active Electronically Scanned Array (AESA) surveillance capability as the primary sensor on the AW101. Formulated on a flat-panel antenna design, Osprey is the world's first lightweight airborne surveillance radar to be built with no moving parts and will provide a full 360 degree field of view for crews.

These radars are at a high technology readiness level (TRL) and are in production for both fixed and rotary wing applications. Its forerunners, the mechanically scanned (M-Scan) and first generation AESA Seaspray radars, have been delivering a high performance surveillance capability to armed forces and paramilitary users for more than forty-five years. This latest

Norwegian AW101-612, 21 March 2017.

asset brings together wide azimuth and elevation electronically scanned (E-Scan) fixed antenna(s) with a compact, state-of-the-art processor and multi-channel receiver.

Norway's Contract Award together with their unique (to date) aircraft specification is certainly a factor likely to attract further potential customers who will consider the versatile helicopter that Norway have procured when considering their own future purchases. Norway had a very clear vision of what aircraft they needed to fulfil the critical role and that is shared by those who might benefit from its service, such as fishermen, oil rig workers, and the public, who are prepared to invest both in the product and the support contracts to achieve it. The significant improvements provided by the AW101 over the legacy Sea King include a 50 per cent increase in payload and a 30 knot increase in cruise speed, as well as harsh weather operations, including continuous icing conditions, and increased mission range, endurance and survivor capacity. Having already built a successful long-term relationship with AW, Norway is confident the manufacturer will continue development of this product as future investment in the AW101 is established.

Royal Navy

The transition of the Merlin from Royal Air Force (RAF) to Royal Navy (RN) service has been a lengthy process that commenced when the first engineers from 846 Naval Air Squadron (NAS) arrived at RAF Benson in early 2012. The whole squadron moved to Benson to learn how to operate and maintain the technologically advanced Merlin HC.3/3A aircraft. With over a decade of operational experience, the RAF had a lot of understanding of the aircraft and its systems to pass onto the navy.

The Merlin was always going to be a step up from the Sea King that operated in navy service. The Sea King was a work horse and with thirty-seven years' service it was very capable, reliable and proven in numerous environments. The Merlin, however, could provide a faster cruise speed, further range and longer endurance. The two side doors of the Merlin also give more flexibility to the aircrew.

Still wearing RAF titles, this RN Merlin HC.3 operates in a confined area on Salisbury Plain, 24 February 2016.

846 NAS return to RNAS
Yeovilton, 26 March 2015.
(Photo: Ian Harding)

The Royal Navy
supporting the Ten
Tors challenge on
Dartmoor, May 2017.
(Photo: Russell Ayre)

Fully operational, 846 NAS returned to RNAS Yeovilton on 26 March 2015 after completing a three-month exercise in Norway. Exercise Clockwork is the Commando Helicopter Force's (CHF) annual chance to test their skills in the harsh winter of northern Norway. Based at a dedicated site on the RNoAF base at Bardufoss, almost 200 miles north of the Arctic Circle, Exercise Clockwork provides one of the toughest environmental challenges for aircraft, air and ground crew.

This high-end training involves many scenarios to test the Merlin aircrew in these harsh conditions. A typical course involves cold weather operations, snow landings, navigational mountain flying and load lifting with the training finishing with tactical flying.

845 NAS, operating alongside 28 AC (Army Co-operative) Squadron, had also been working up to operational status at RAF Benson. Operational status declared, 28 Squadron disbanded and 845 NAS re-joined 846 NAS back at RNAS Yeovilton, marking the end of Merlin flying from RAF Benson.

With the squadron active, the CHF Merlin unit training could increase. Being a 'Commando' squadron working predominantly with the Royal Marines, 845 NAS took part

Above: The third
HC.3 built for the
RAF now operates
with the Royal Navy.
(Photo: Paul Harvey)

Right: A fantastic
and unusual view of
a Royal Navy Merlin
dispensing flares.
(Photo: Paul Harvey)

in Exercise Black Alligator in the United States. Based at Marine Corps Air Ground Combat Centre Twentynine Palms in California, this exercise provides the most action-packed dry heat live-firing training Royal Marines get anywhere in the world.

An important element of this exercise incorporated an Environmental Qualification phase for aircrew. This ensured the basics of operating in such a harsh environment were fully grasped by the squadron. During this phase aircrew completed dust landings, load lifting training and formation flying both during the day and night. Once completed crews then consolidated their skills and also conducted tasking in the form of troop drills with UK and foreign troops during the exercise.

Troops from the 2nd Royal Gurkha Rifles, part of 16 AAB, board a Merlin from the Royal Navy on Salisbury Plain during Exercise Merlin Storm 1-17. (Photo: Mick Holland)

Exercise Black Alligator 2015. (Photo: Joe Copalman)

The Merlin HC.3 was designed for the battlefield, so to meet future operational requirements within the Royal Navy's Commando Helicopter Force (CHF), the HC.3/3A fleet would eventually require upgrade and modernisation to meet the Royal Navy's operational maritime requirements. As a result, the Ministry of Defence announced during January 2014 that AgustaWestland (AW) (now Leonardo Helicopters) had been awarded the contract to convert twenty-five of the former RAF Merlin HC.3/3A (nineteen HC.3 and six HC.3A) helicopters for maritime operations. Valued at approximately £455 million, the Merlin Life Sustainment Programme (MLSP) has two primary elements. Firstly, a life sustainment package to resolve legacy obsolescence out to the type's planned 2030 Out of Service Date (OSD). Secondly, a ship optimisation package to enable the aircraft to operate more effectively from ships in the maritime environment. The programme is under way with the objective of delivering the first upgraded Commando Merlin to CHF at Royal Naval Air Station Yeovilton in Somerset in early 2018. The first HC.4 made its initial flight on 24 October 2016. The first HC.4A is expected to fly in early 2019.

Exercise Black Alligator 2015. (Photo: Joe Copalman)

Phase 1 of this programme saw seven aircraft converted to 'interim' HC.3 (also referred to as iMk 3) standard to enable the CHF to maintain embarked operations and to bridge the capability gap between the Sea King OSD set for March 2016 and the service introduction of the Merlin HC.4/HC4A in early 2018.

Key differences are:

Folding main rotor head (non-folding tail). Ground crew will control this operation;
New fast roping point, modified undercarriage for deck operations;
New aircraft lashing points for deck security.

Phase 2 of this programme involves the conversion of twenty-five aircraft to full HC.4/HC.4A standard. Additional modifications made to the I HC.3 focus primarily on the upgrade of the cockpit and ship optimisation. The modifications are as follows:

Key features of avionics design include upgraded Aircraft Management and Mission Computers (AMMCs), General Dynamics Tactical Processor (derived from the AW159 Wildcat), five 10 in. x 8 in. General Electric integrated display units (IDUs), three BARCO touch screen units (TSUs) for controlling the aircraft's systems and mission equipment, two cursor control devices for cursor control of the tactical displays, a new communication suite (derived from Merlin HM.2 Communication Control and Intercom System) with a specific radio fit for the HC.4/HC.4A requirement, an I-Band Transponder System navigational equipment (again similar to the HM.2 but integrated into the aircraft avionics);

Integrated Defensive Aids Suite with additional chaff dispensers mounted in the roof of the aircraft;

Additional systems for civil airspace operational requirements. Includes a Civil Twin Global Positioning System, Dual VHF Omni Directional Range/Instrument Landing System;

Folding main rotor head and tail pylon which is cockpit controlled as per HM.2;

Fast roping and abseiling beam.

The HC.4 Initial Release to Service is scheduled for quarter 1 2018 with the first aircraft due to be delivered to the Royal Navy and the CHF at Yeovilton immediately post issue of the Release to Service. All twenty-five helicopters are scheduled to be delivered by December 2020 with Full Operational Capability also set for the end of 2020.

The upgraded Merlins will continue to be supported through the existing Integrated Merlin Operational Support (IMOS) contract, which has been in place since 2006.

The first upgraded HC.4, ZJ122, for the RN, 26 November 2016.

ZJ127, the second Merlin HC.4, on a test flight, 21 March 2017.

The first HC.4 demonstrates the main and tail rotor fold at Westland's. (Photo: Leonardo Helicopters)

846 NAS conducting familiarisation training with the Dartmoor Search and Rescue Team (DSRT) ahead of the annual Ten Tors Challenge held in May. 19 April 2017. (Photo: Shaun Schofield)

Head of Government and State Transport (VVIP)

The use of the AW101 in Very, Very Important Person (VVIP) configuration confirms the versatility of the AW101. Lavishly furnished throughout, the cabin has low noise and vibration with air conditioning. The 6.1 ft (1.83 m) cabin height provides stand-up headroom. The 8.6 ft (2.49 m) width provides space for luxury seats, in-flight information and in-flight entertainment. A typical VVIP AW101 may include staff seats, secure communications, washroom, shower, medical equipment and ballistic protection with forward air-stair door for VVIP ingress and egress. Other features may include a defensive aids suite comprising Radar Warning Receiver, Laser Warning System, Missile Approach Warning System, Countermeasures Dispensing System, and Directed Infra-Red Countermeasures.

During August 2013, the AW101 VVIP company demonstrator was on static show at the International Aviation and Space Salon (MAKS) in Zhukovsky, Russia.

This VVIP AW101 has also transported the British Prime Minister David Cameron and the UK delegation during the two-day NATO summit in 2014, which was attended by more than sixty world leaders. In May 2017, the company VVIP demonstrator was leased to the Italian government to provide transportation during the forty-third G7 summit, held in Taormina, Sicily.

The G7 summit is a forum that plays an important role in shaping global responses to global challenges, complementing the global economic coordination carried out by the G20. It brings together leaders from Canada, France, Germany, Italy, Japan, the United Kingdom, the United States and the EU.

Above: Company demonstrator ZR339, an AW101 Mk.641 in VIP configuration, flying a test flight as 'Westland12' on 3 April 2017.

Left: VVIP luxury on board ZR339, the AW101 Mk 641 demonstrator.

VVIP luxury on board ZR339, the AW101 Mk 641 demonstrator.

Company demonstrator AW101 Mk 641 sat on the apron at Newquay. (Photo: Peter Mitrovich)

CHAPTER ELEVEN

Magical Merlin at Thirty

Over the last thirty years, the EH/AW101 has seen several mergers of its parent companies. Automotive and aerospace firm GKN bought into Westland during 1988 and took full control in 1995. Agusta was absorbed by Finmeccanica in 1992. In 1998 GKN and Finemeccanica announced that they had started negotiations to create a joint venture company by combining their respective helicopter companies, Westland and Agusta. The company, AgustaWestland, was formed in 2000. Finmeccanica decided in 2016 to consolidate their subsidiary companies to form one large company. The aim of this was to make the group more efficient by bringing together research, marketing and sales, engineering, procurement and strategies.

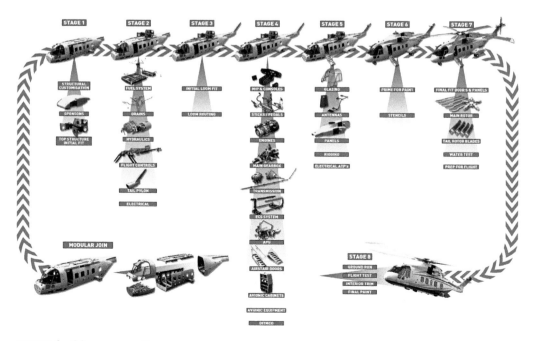

AW101 build sequence diagram.

Early on in the build stage, this AW101 was on show at the Westland Centenary family open day, July 2015. 100 years of aircraft building in Yeovil, Somerset.

A view of the intricate wiring inside the cockpit. (Photo: Leonardo Helicopters)

The company then began a rebranding operation, with the shareholders approving a new company name on 28 April 2016. On 1 January 2017, Finmeccanica officially became Leonardo. The name Leonardo was inspired by the Italian Leonardo da Vinci, a polymath who is sometimes credited with the invention of the helicopter.

The AW101 is the most modern and advanced medium-lift helicopter available today. It has a proven performance in service, operating in all environments from the Arctic to the Antarctic, which has created an increasing demand for production. The EH/AW101 is a global success, with nearly 220 orders placed, including the nine pre-production aircraft.

The term 'maturity' conjures many connotations, but the AW101 is now proven as evidenced by well over 325,000 operational flight hours in some of the world's toughest environments – long range SAR (Canada/Portugal) and Afghanistan to name two extremes. Coupled with world-class technological expansion at Leonardo and within AW, the AW101's future is assured at the cutting edge of design.

Is today's AW101 a new or old aircraft? While the aircraft retains the same basic external design, its multi-role capability and internal structures and systems have developed to the point where it is definitely a new generation helicopter. Think of it as 'thirty years young' and the good news is there's yet more 'wizardry' to come from Merlin!

Wiring loom installation down through the fuselage. (Photo: Leonardo Helicopters)

The future 'Crowsnest' AW101. (Photo: Leonardo Helicopters)

The futuristic-looking cockpit on board the AW101 HM.2. (Photo: Leonardo Helicopters)

'Westland 01', Andy Strachan, testing the latest SAR AW101 for Norway.

The Italian Air Force ordered fifteen examples of the HH-101A Caesar to replace the Sikorsky HH-3 Pelican for personnel recovery and Special Forces operations.

Above: HH-101A as the sun sets at the RNAS Merryfield open day, 2015.

Left: Kicking up a storm, 846 NAS return to RNAS Yeovilton. (Chris Shaw www.shaw-arts.co.uk)